NATASHA JONES

ADULT COLORING BOOK

FUN & RELAXING MANDALAS & MORE

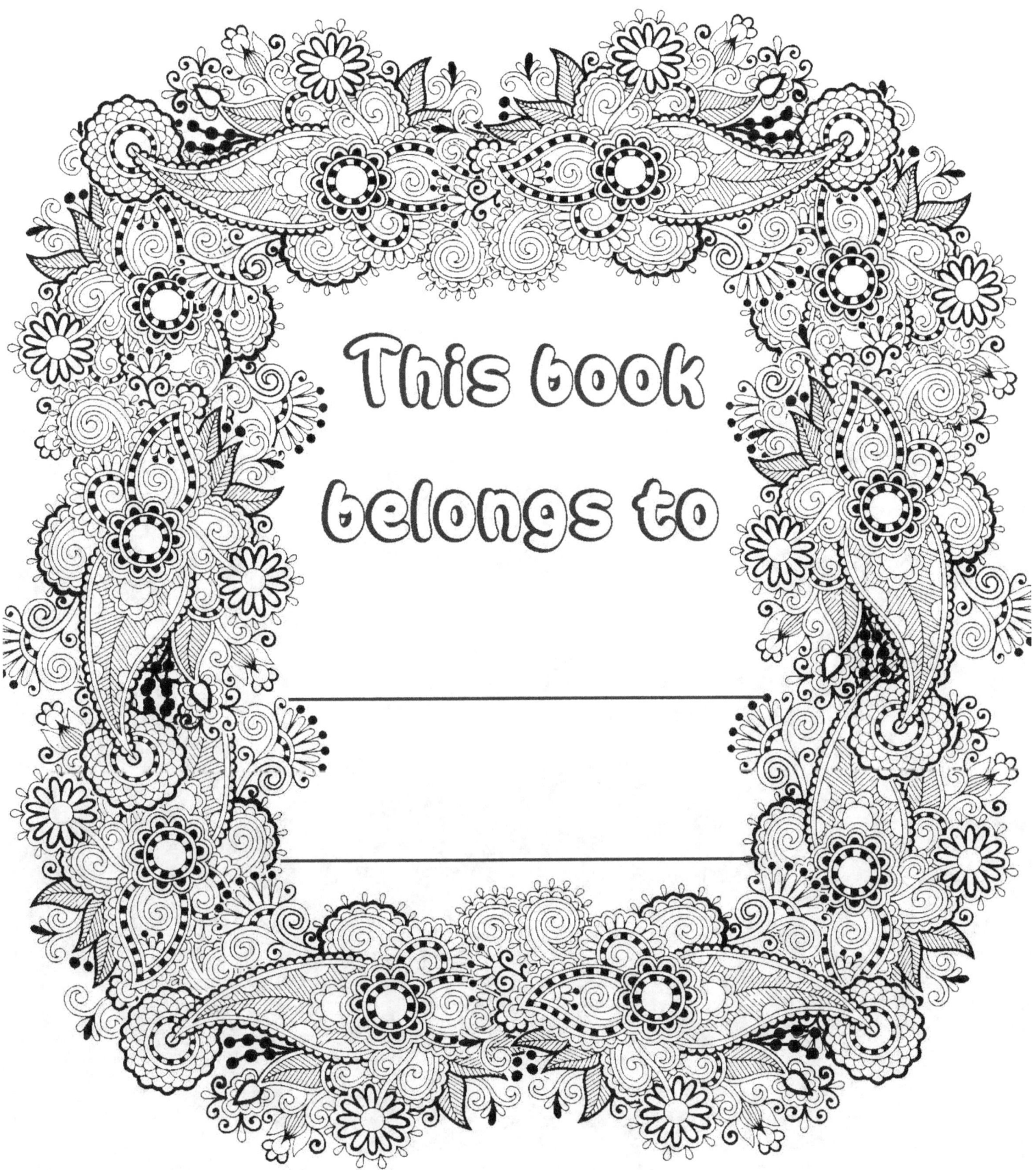

This book belongs to

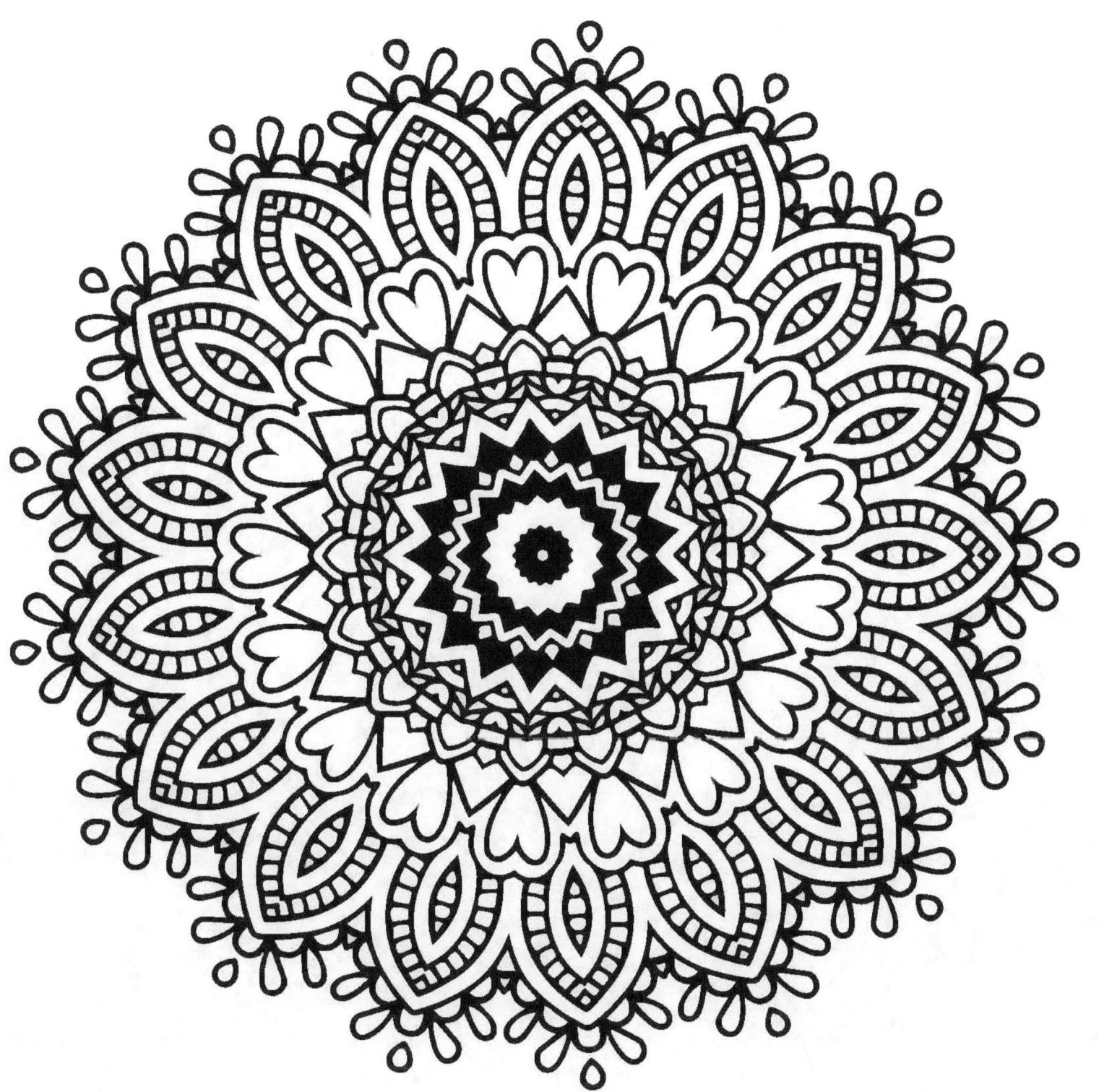

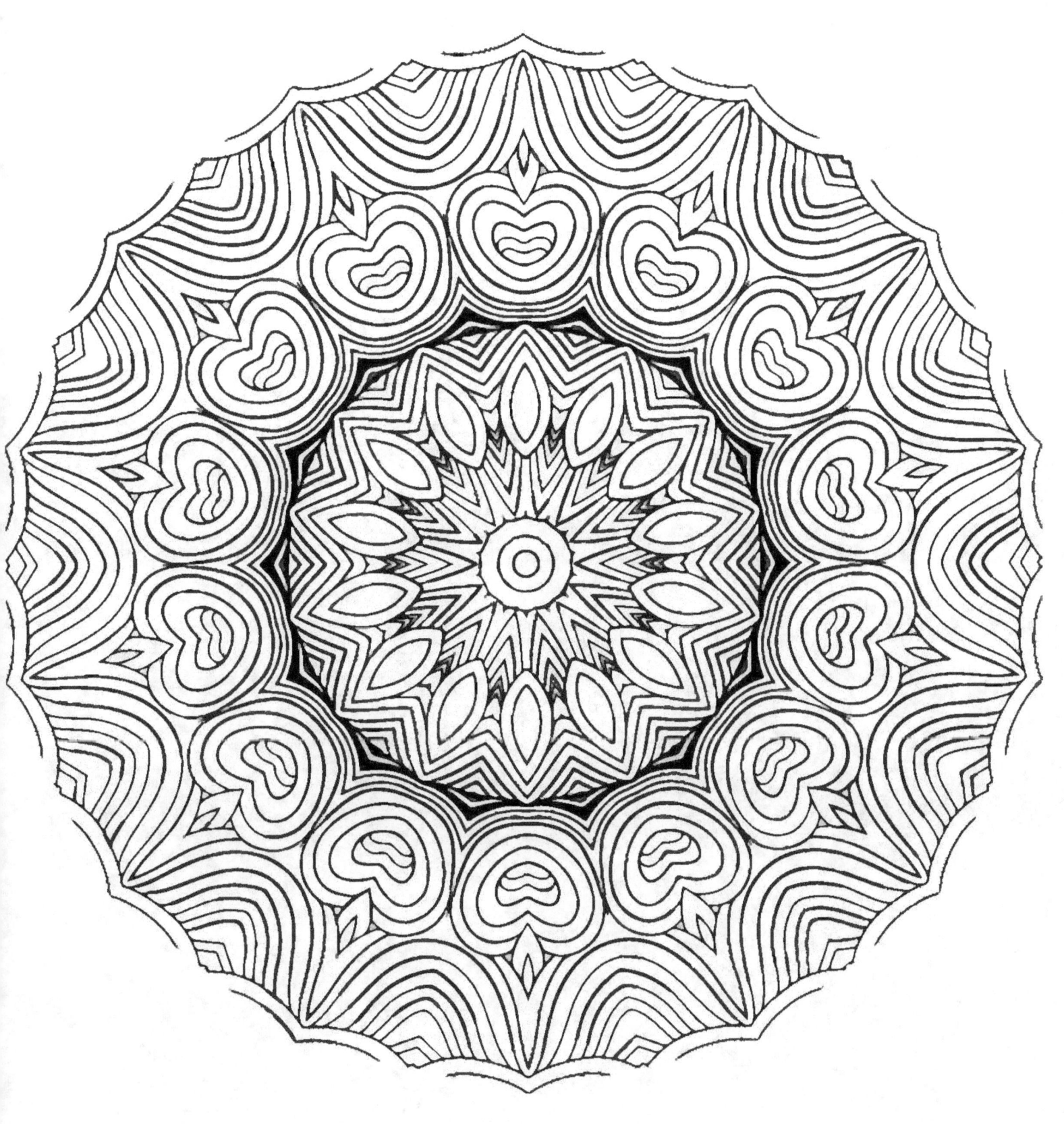

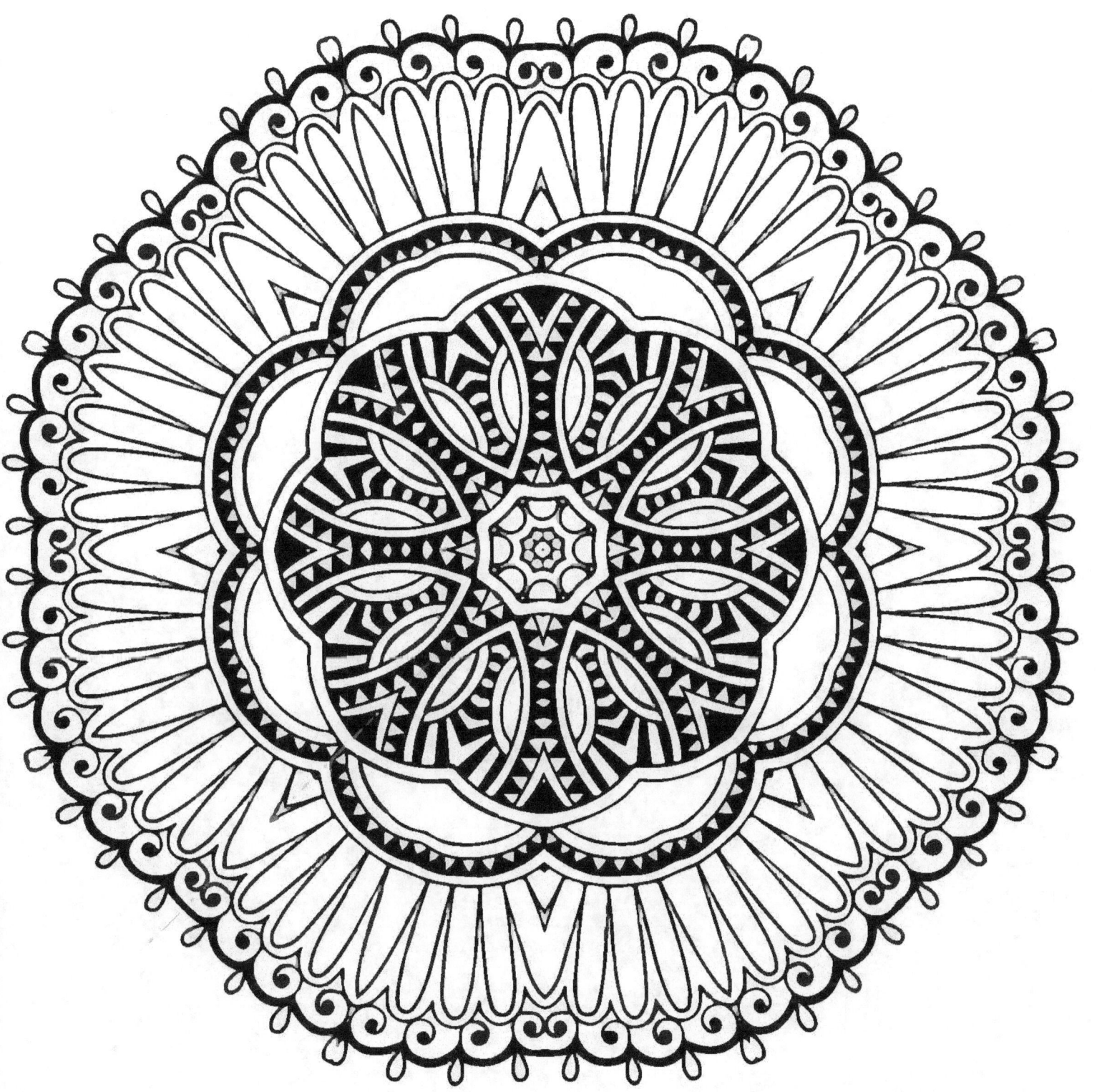

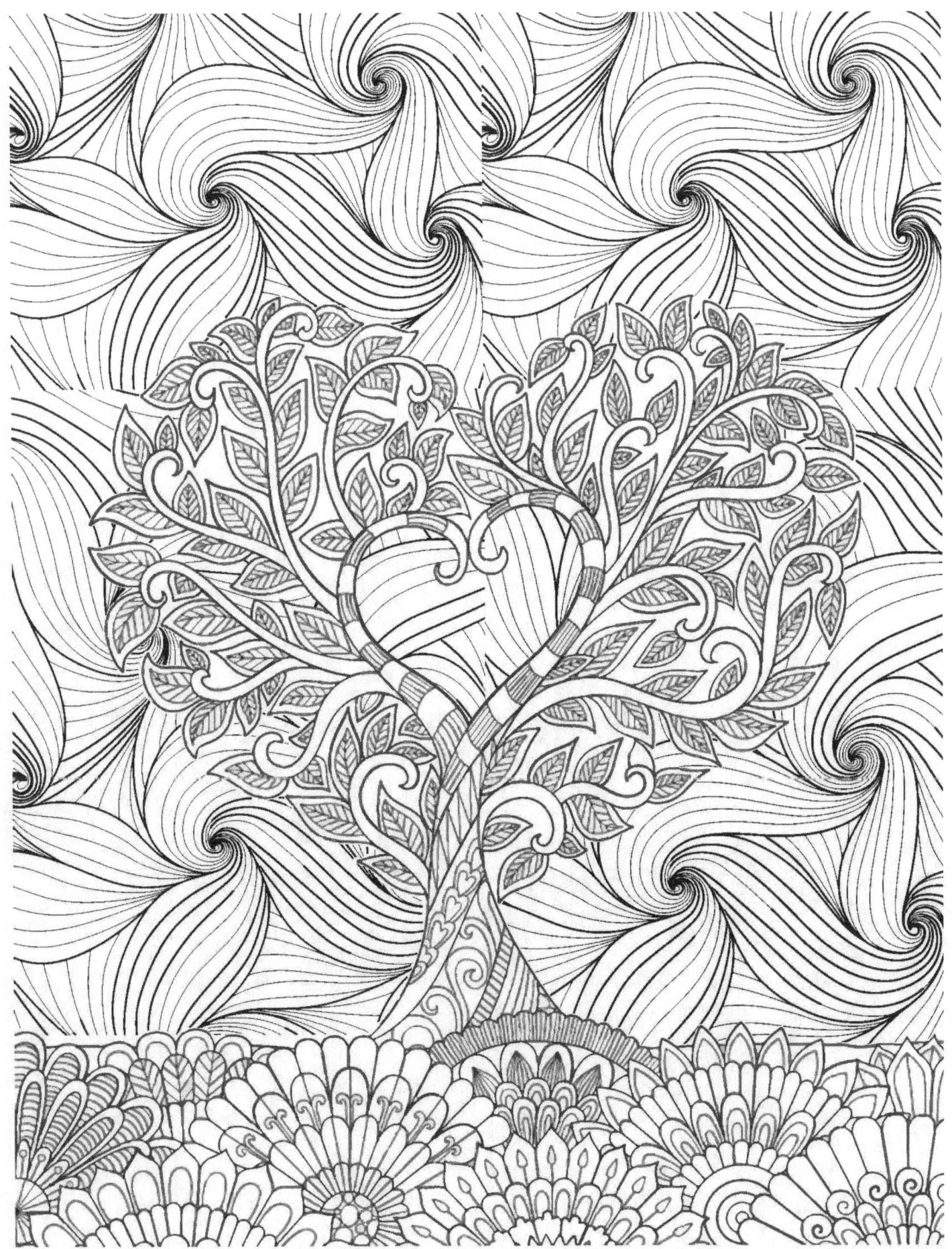

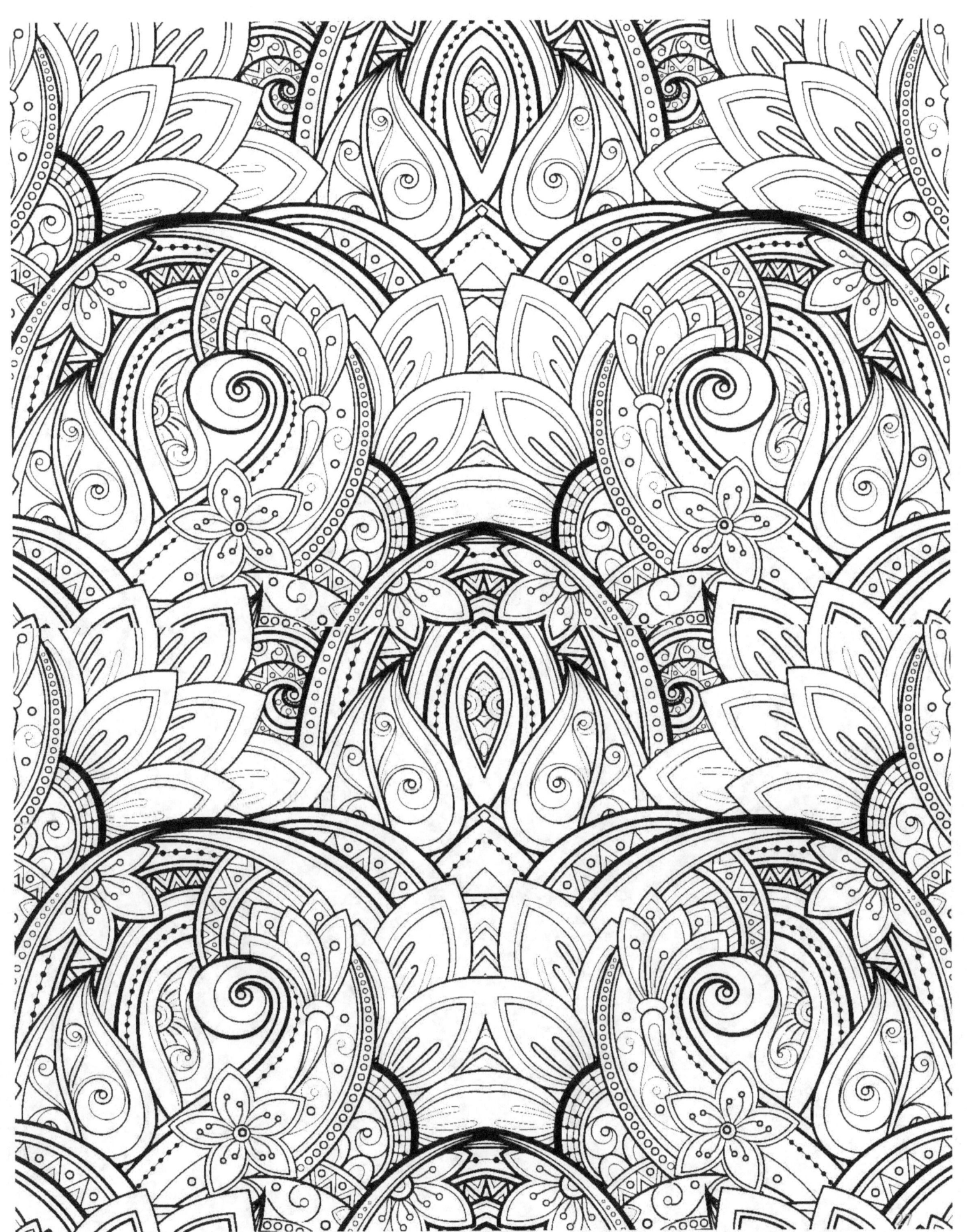

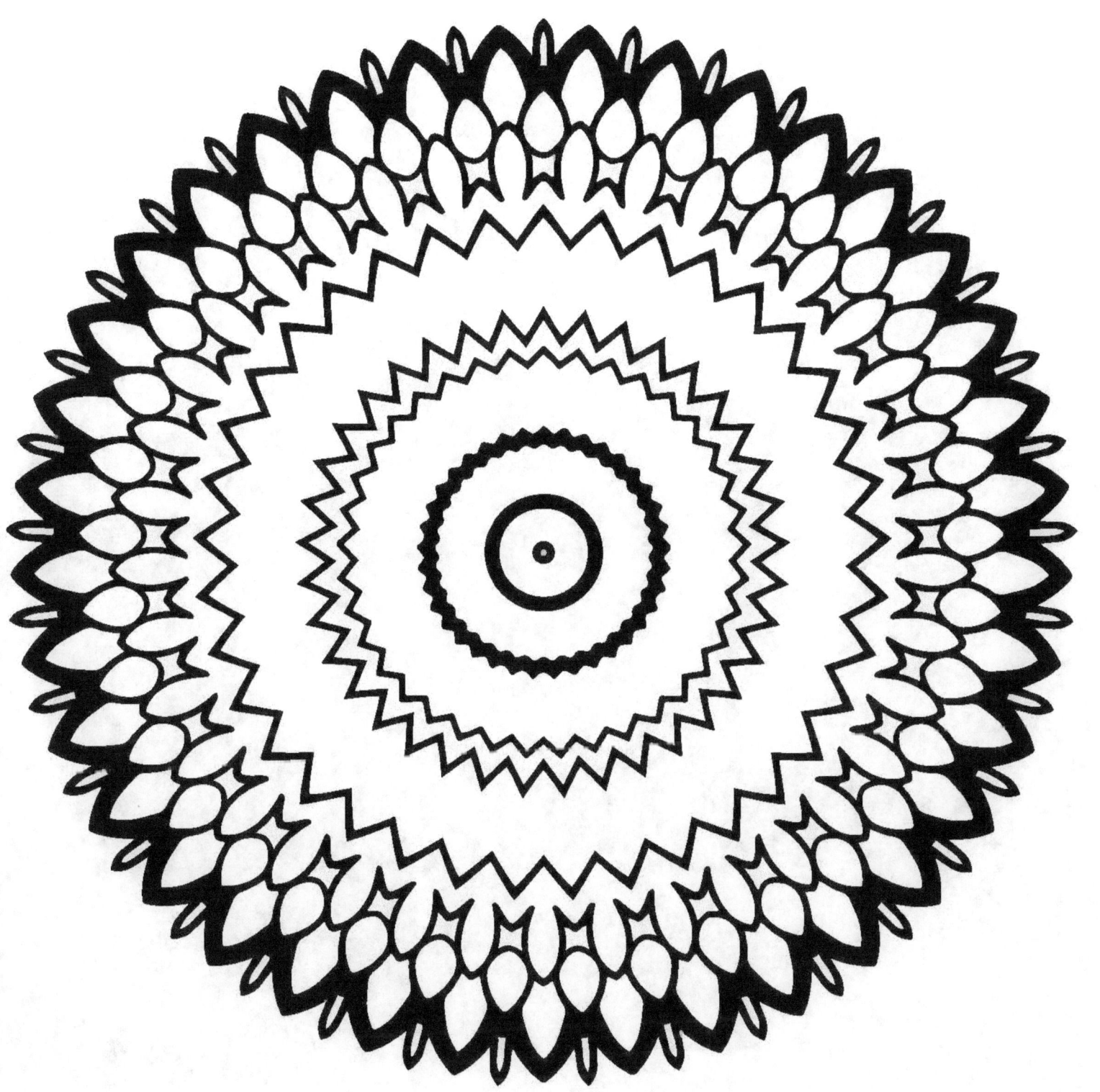

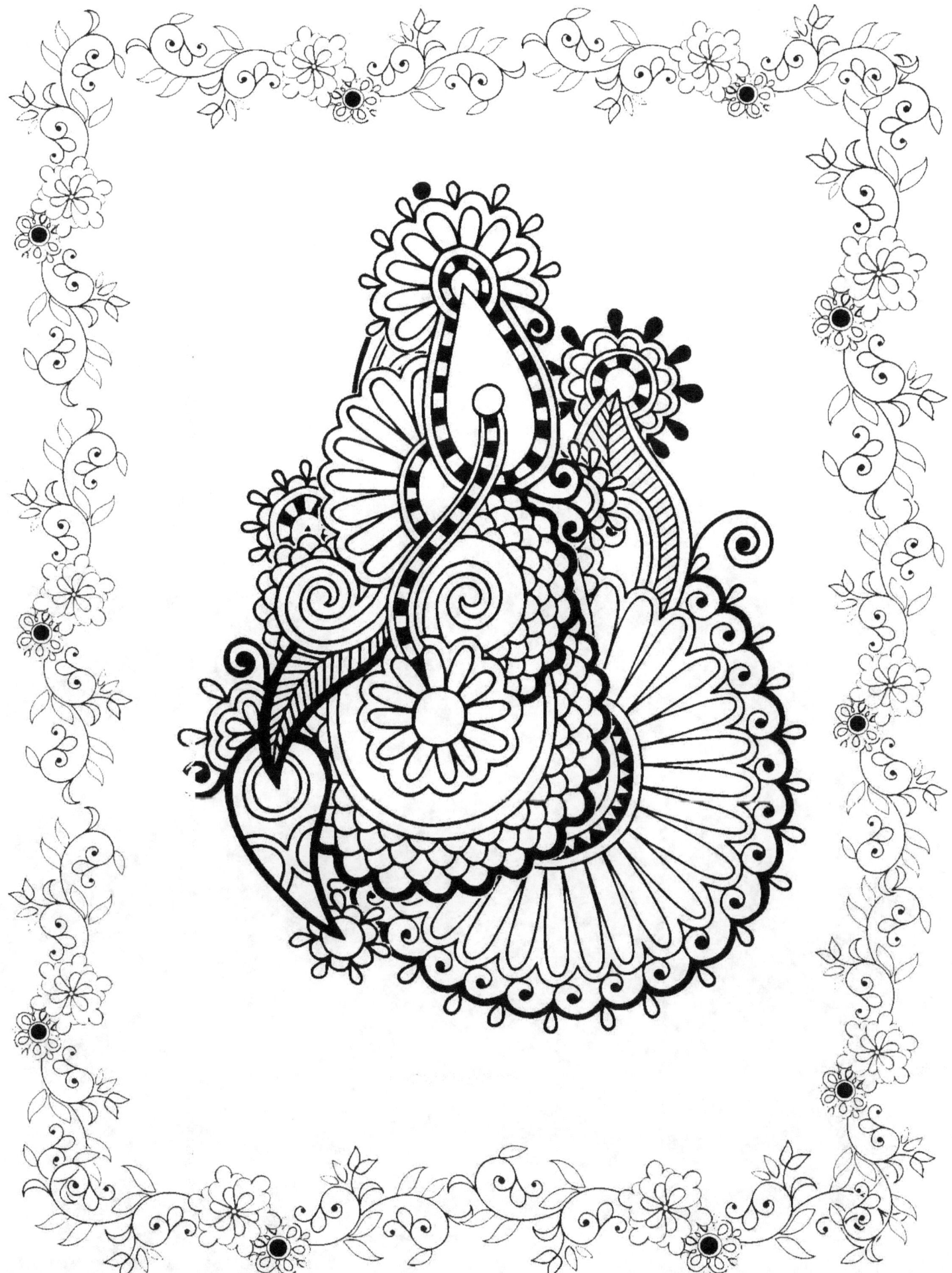

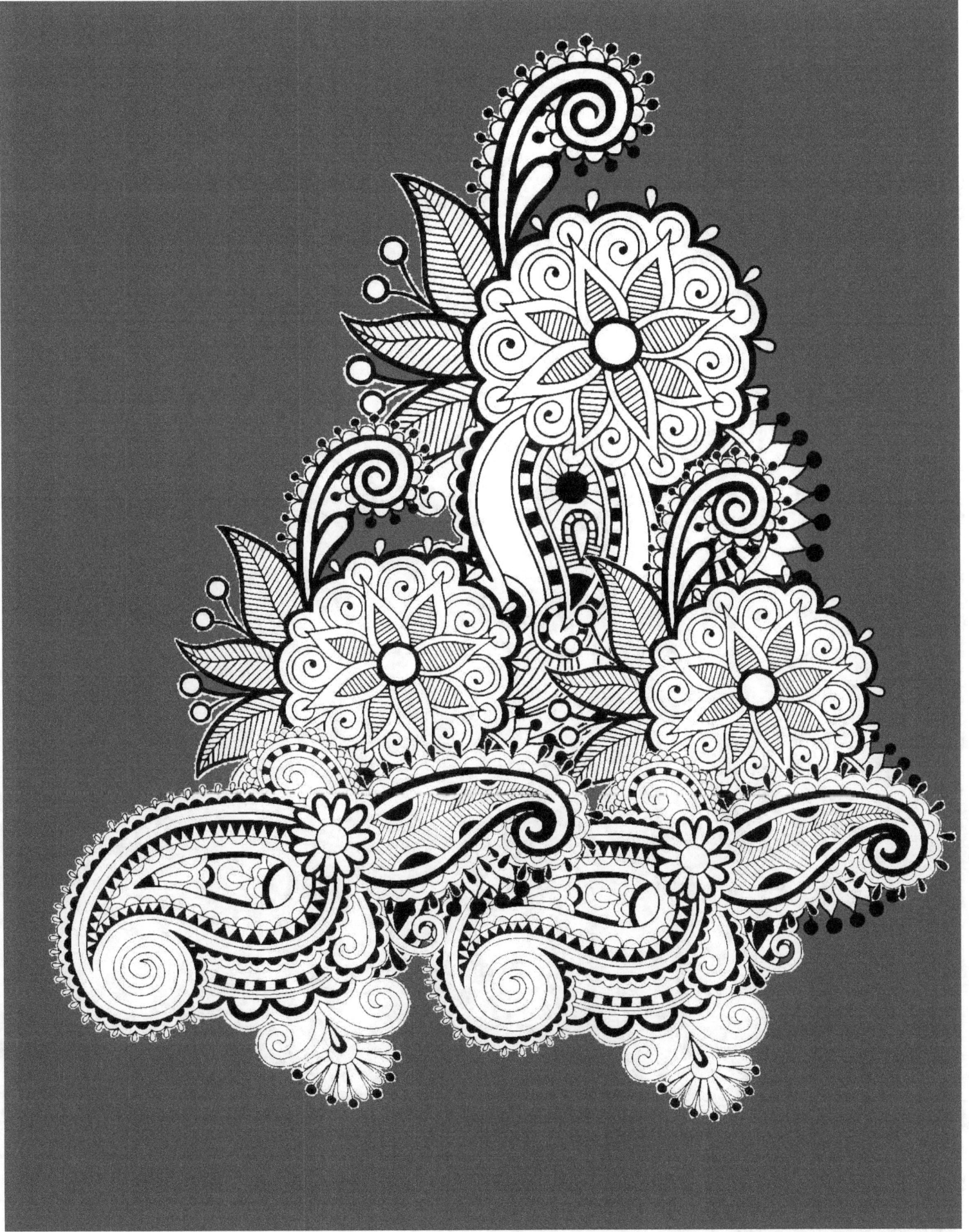

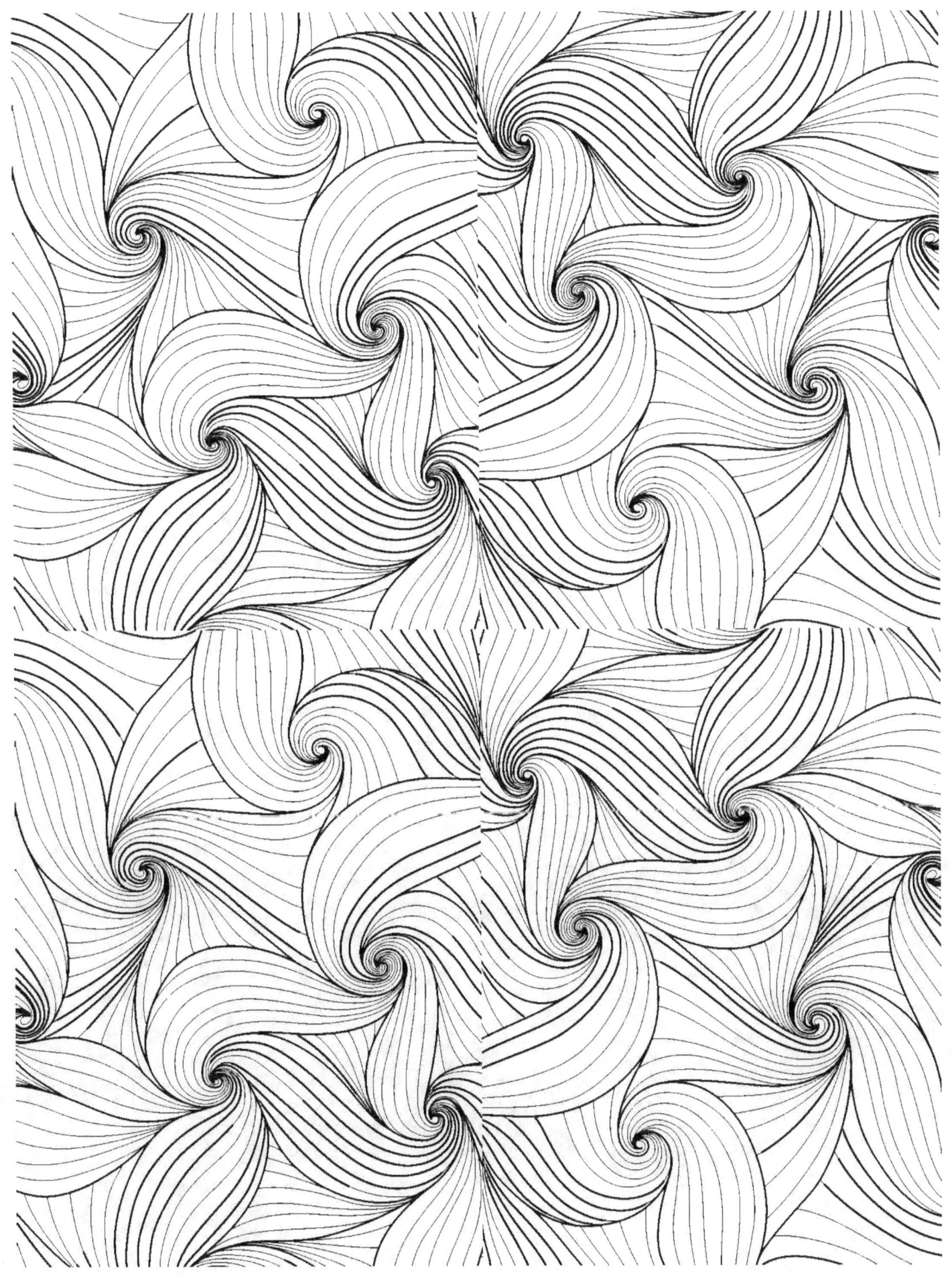

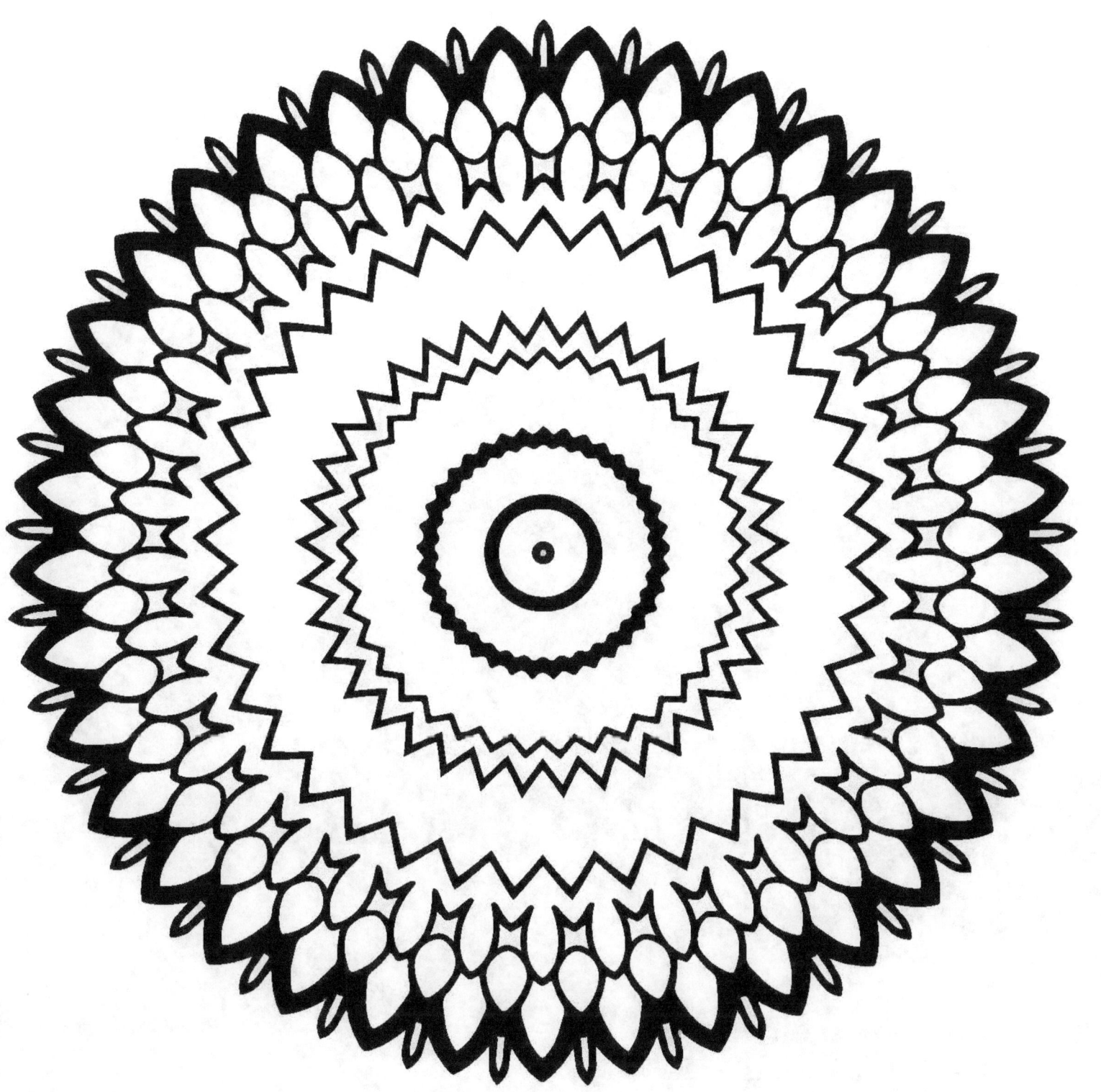

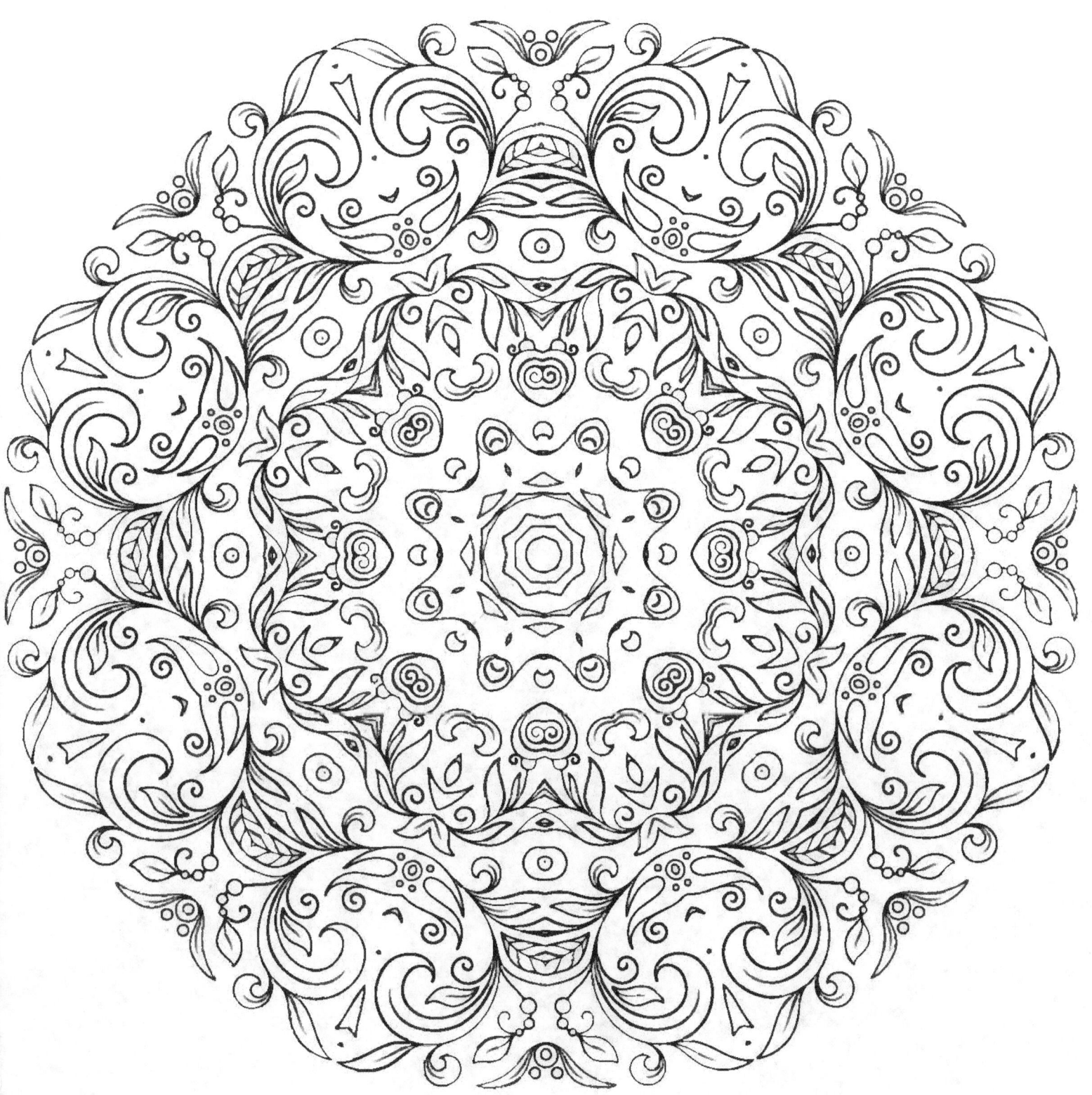

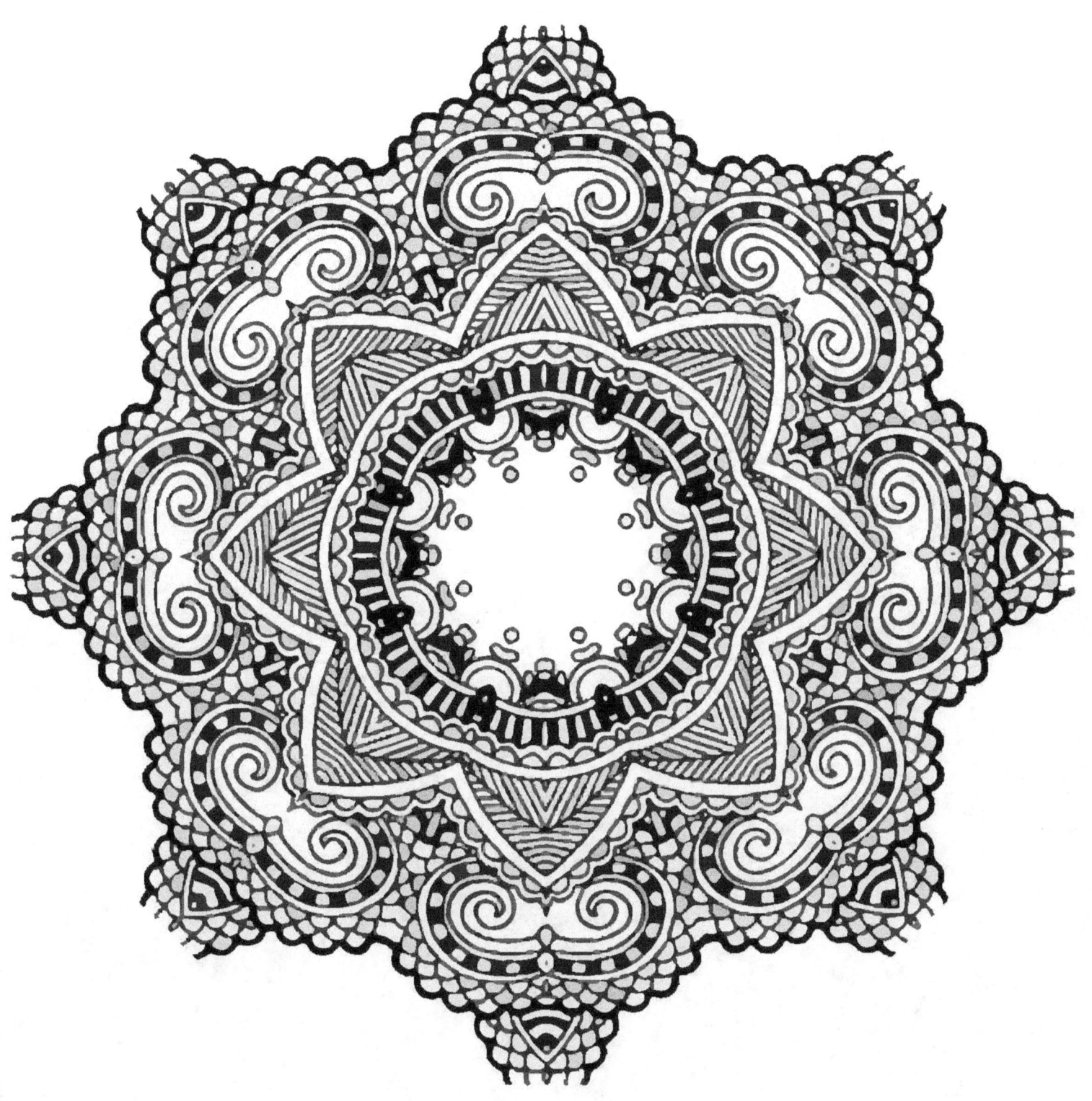

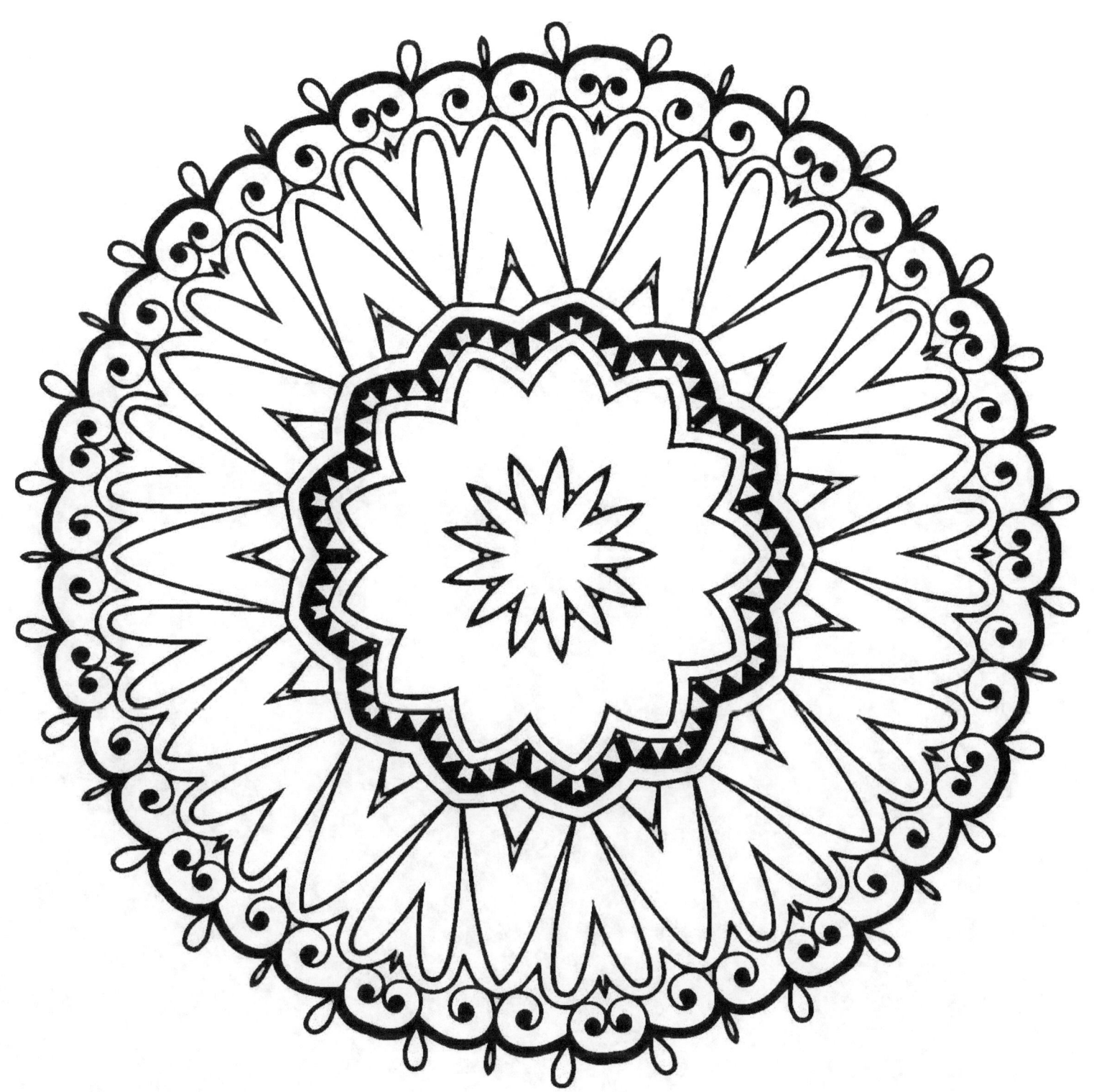

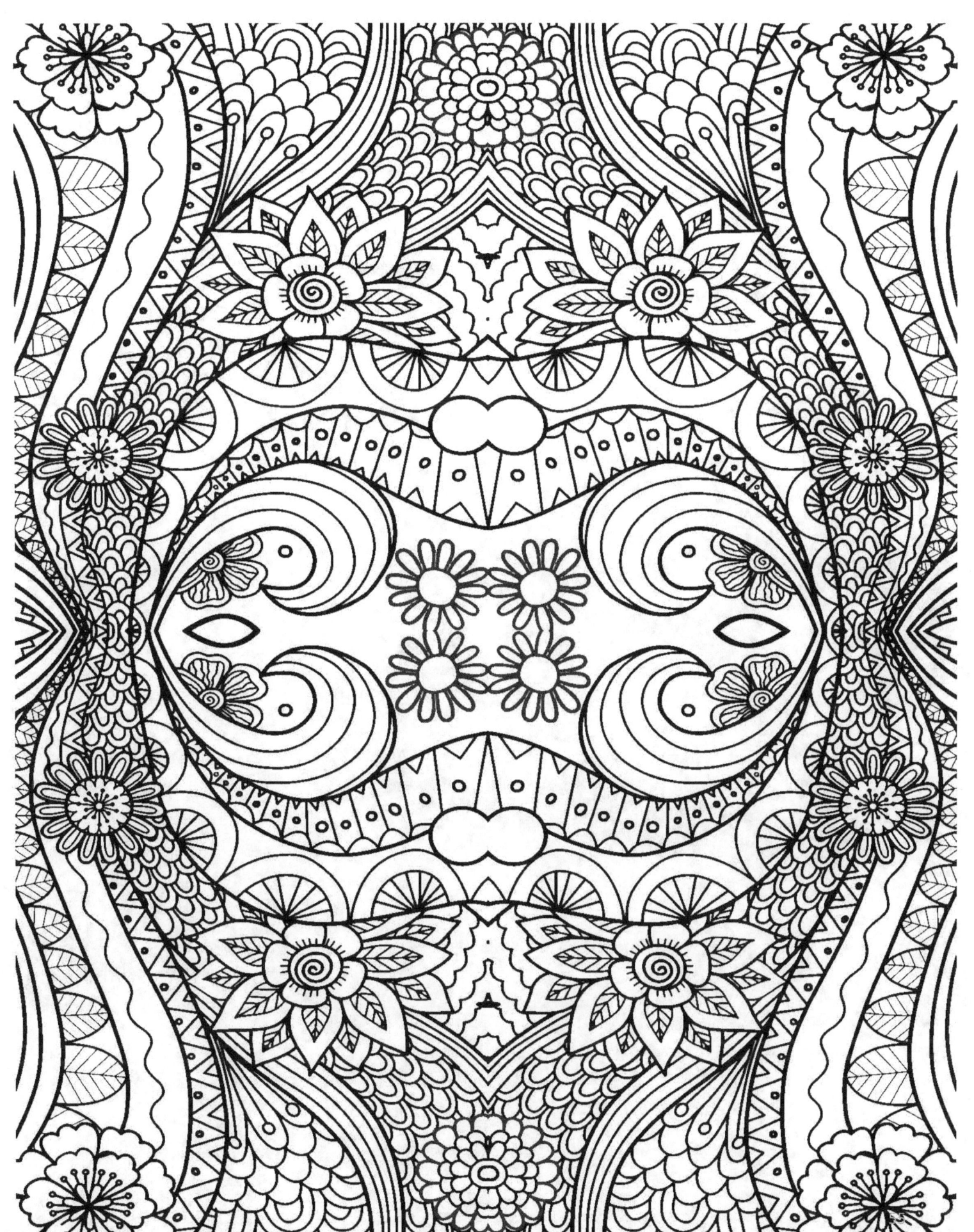

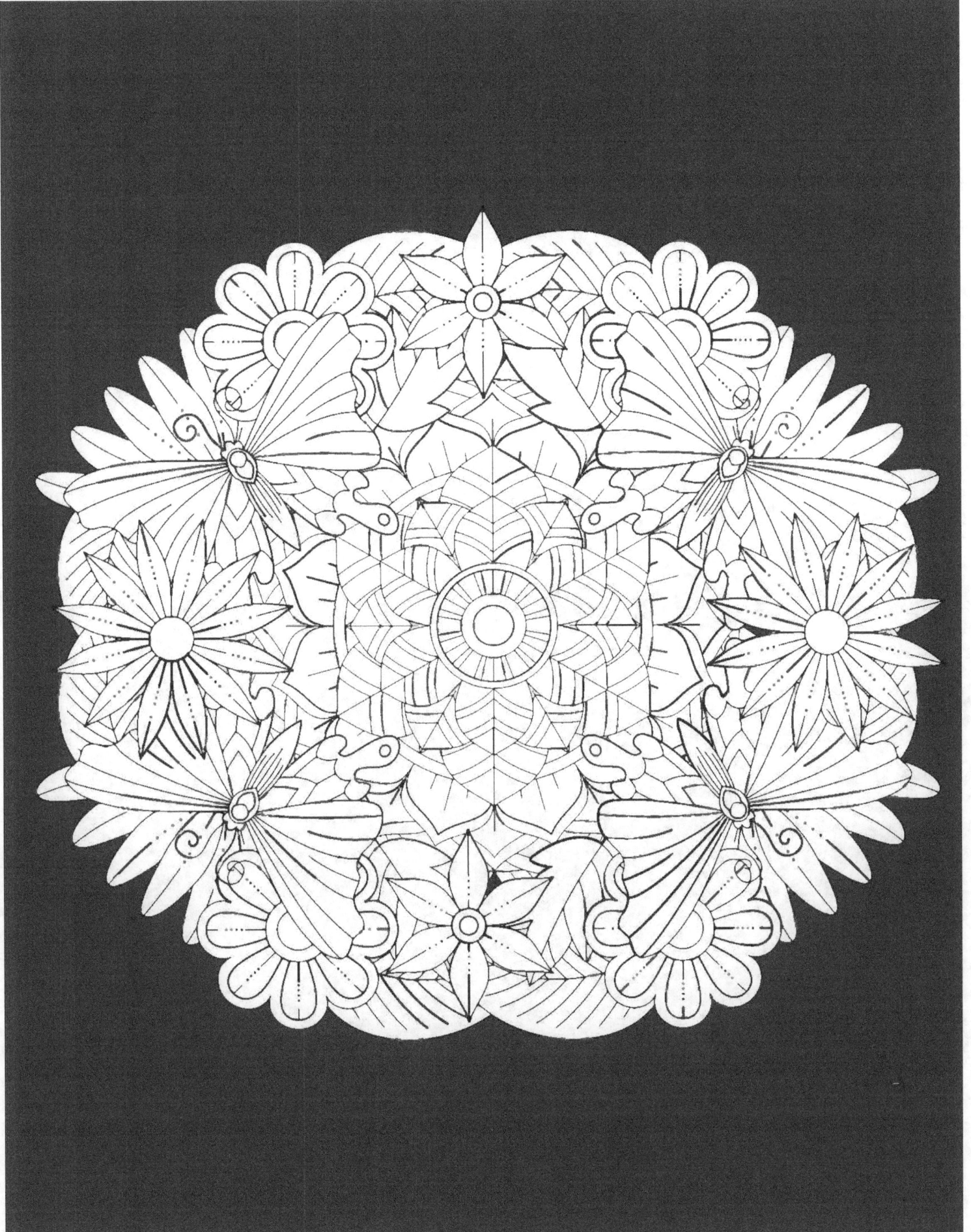

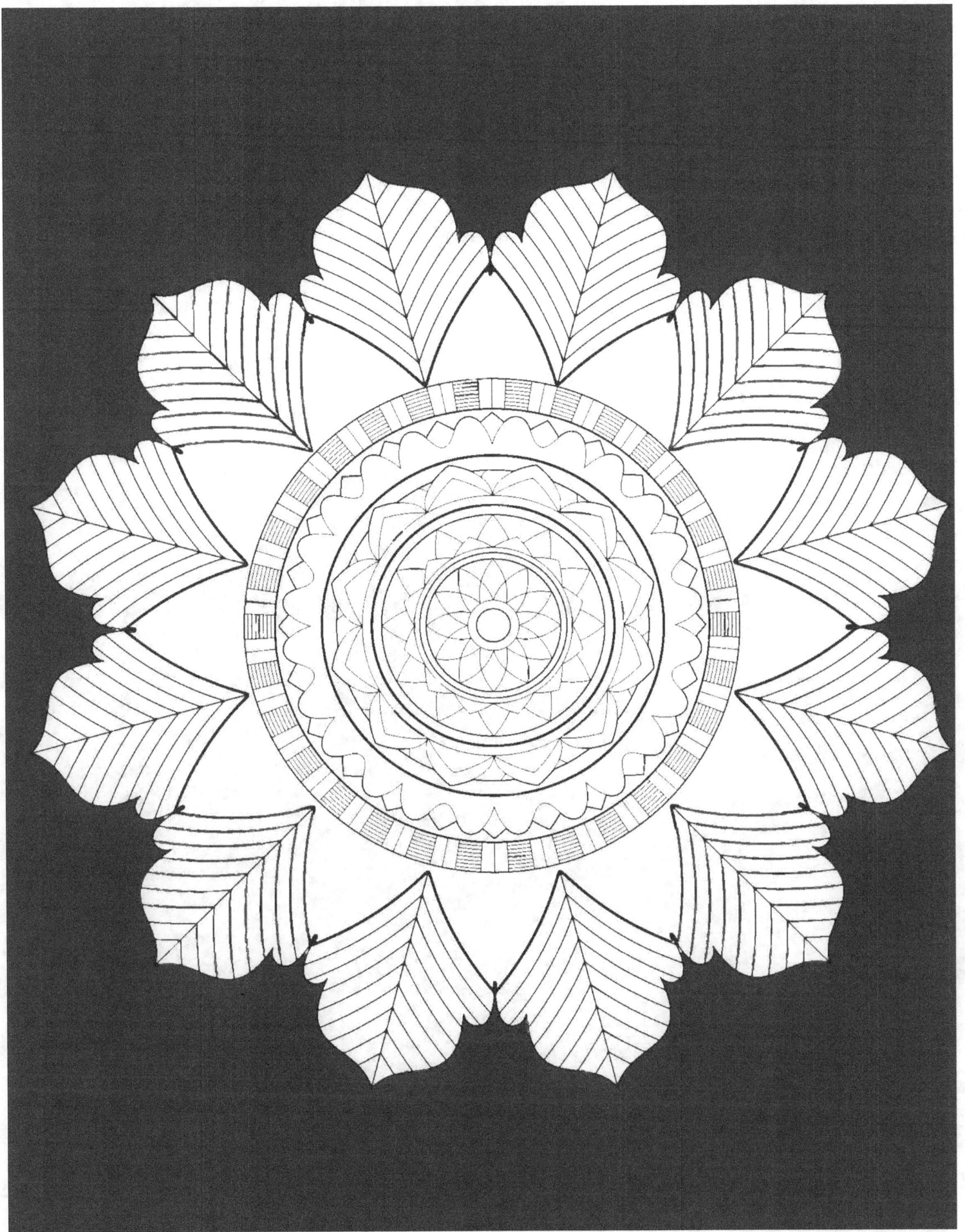

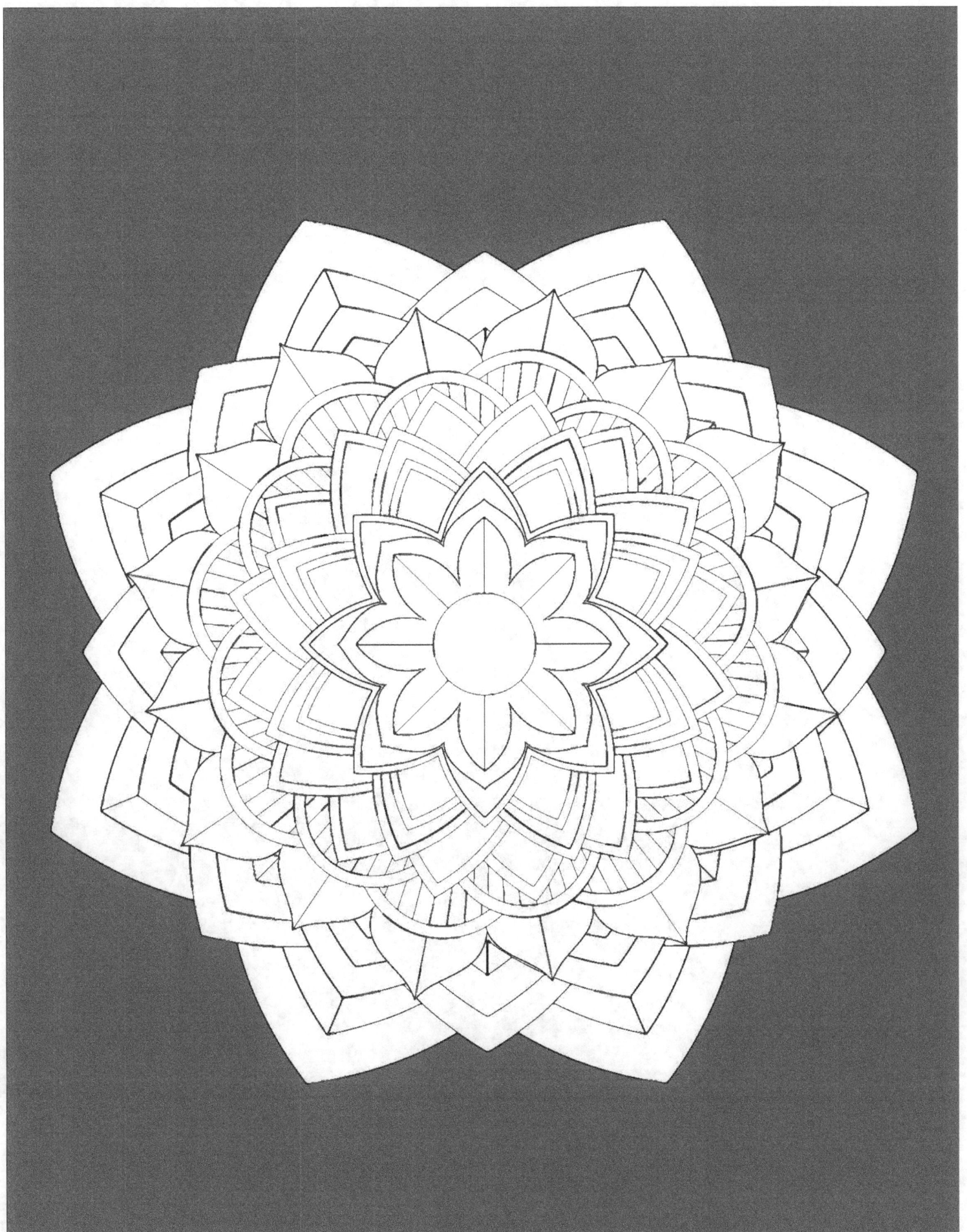

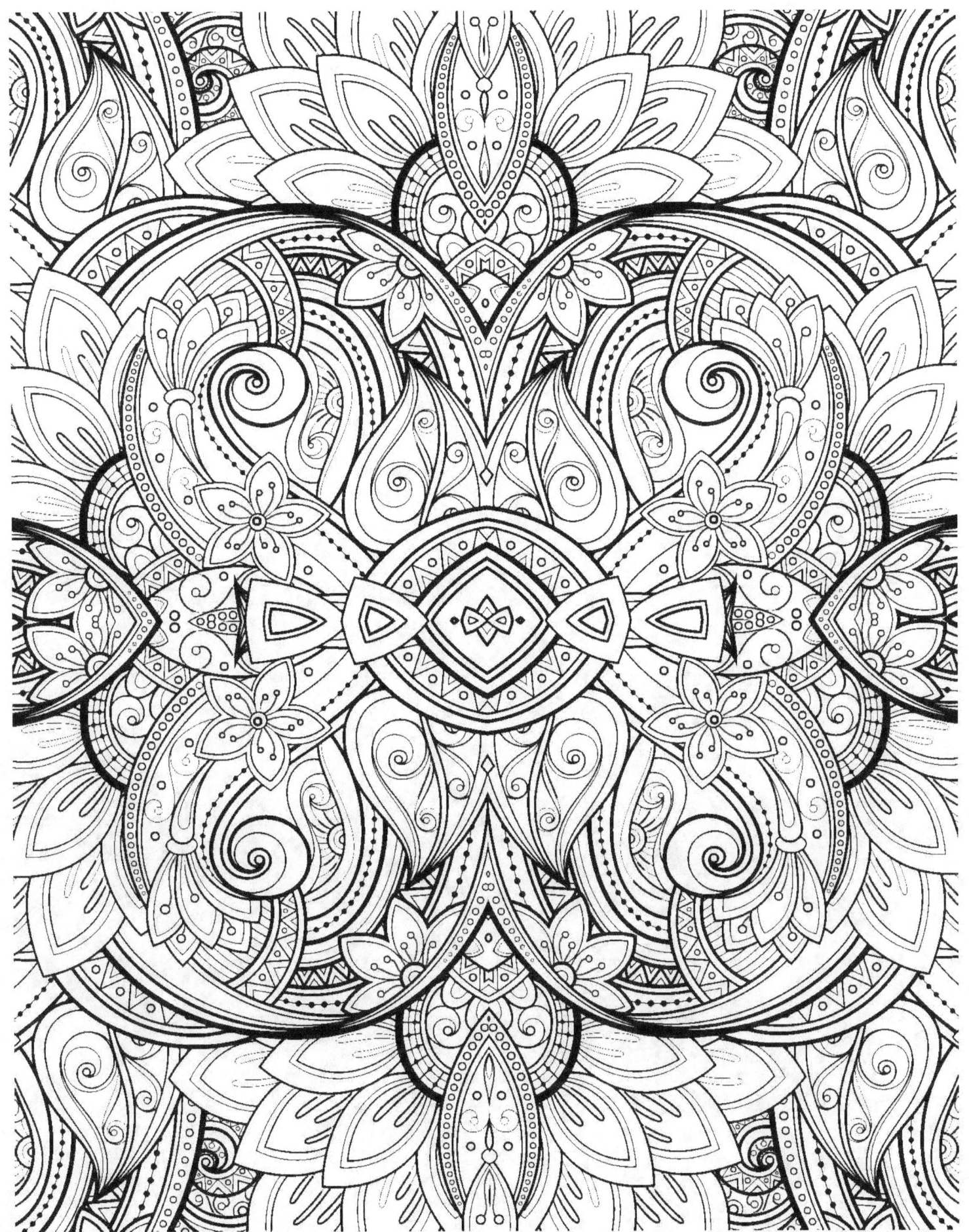

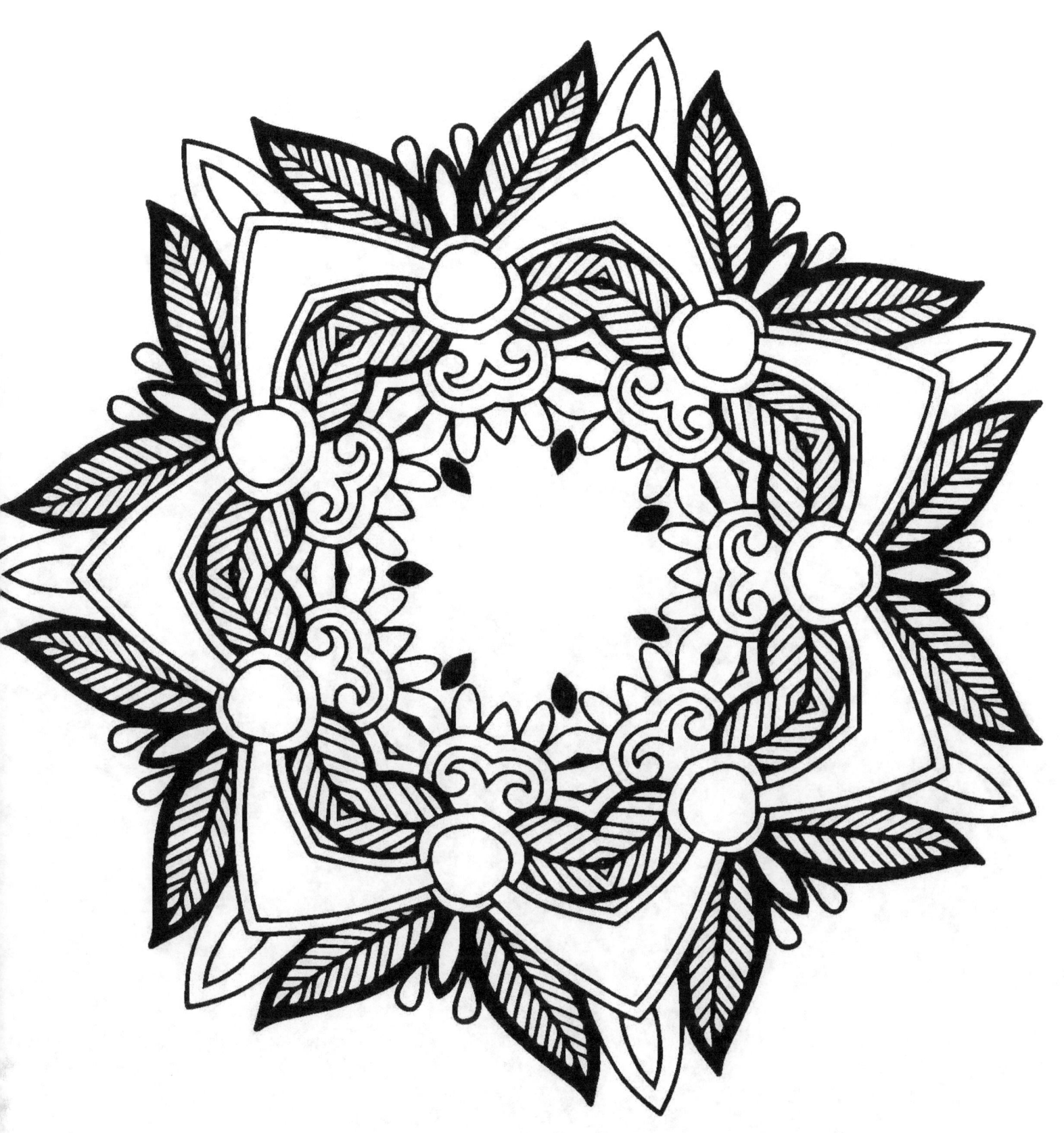

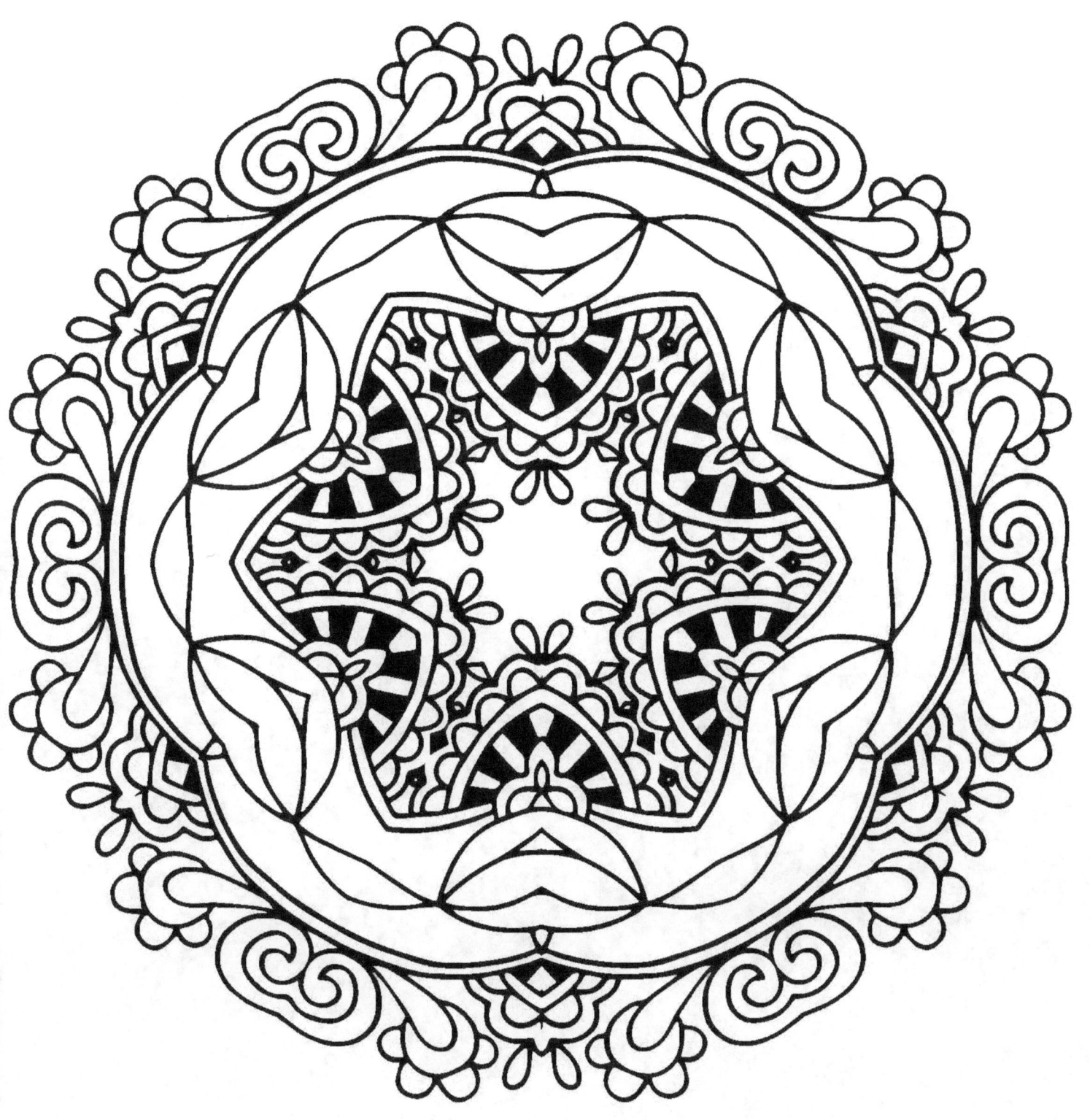

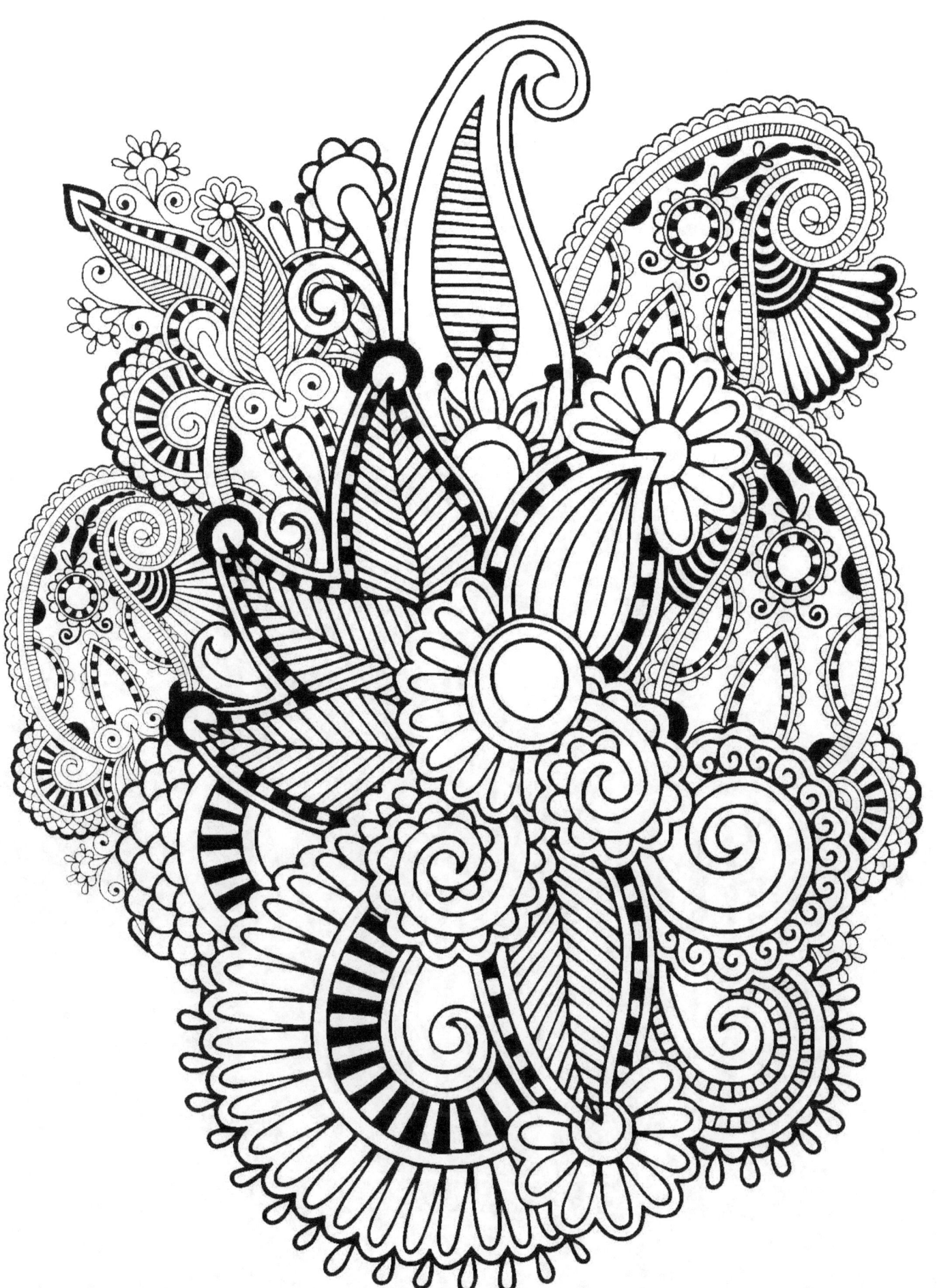

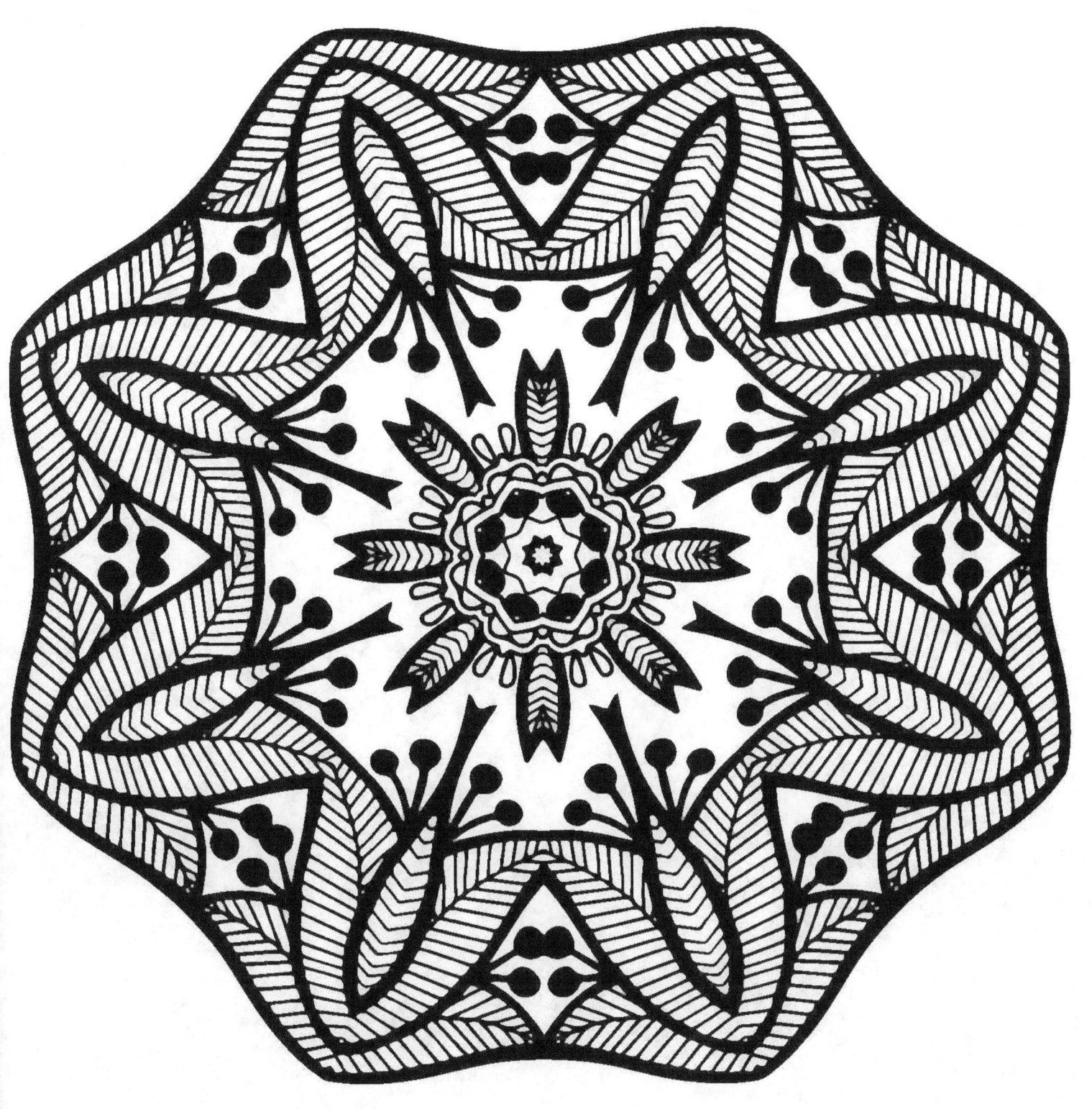

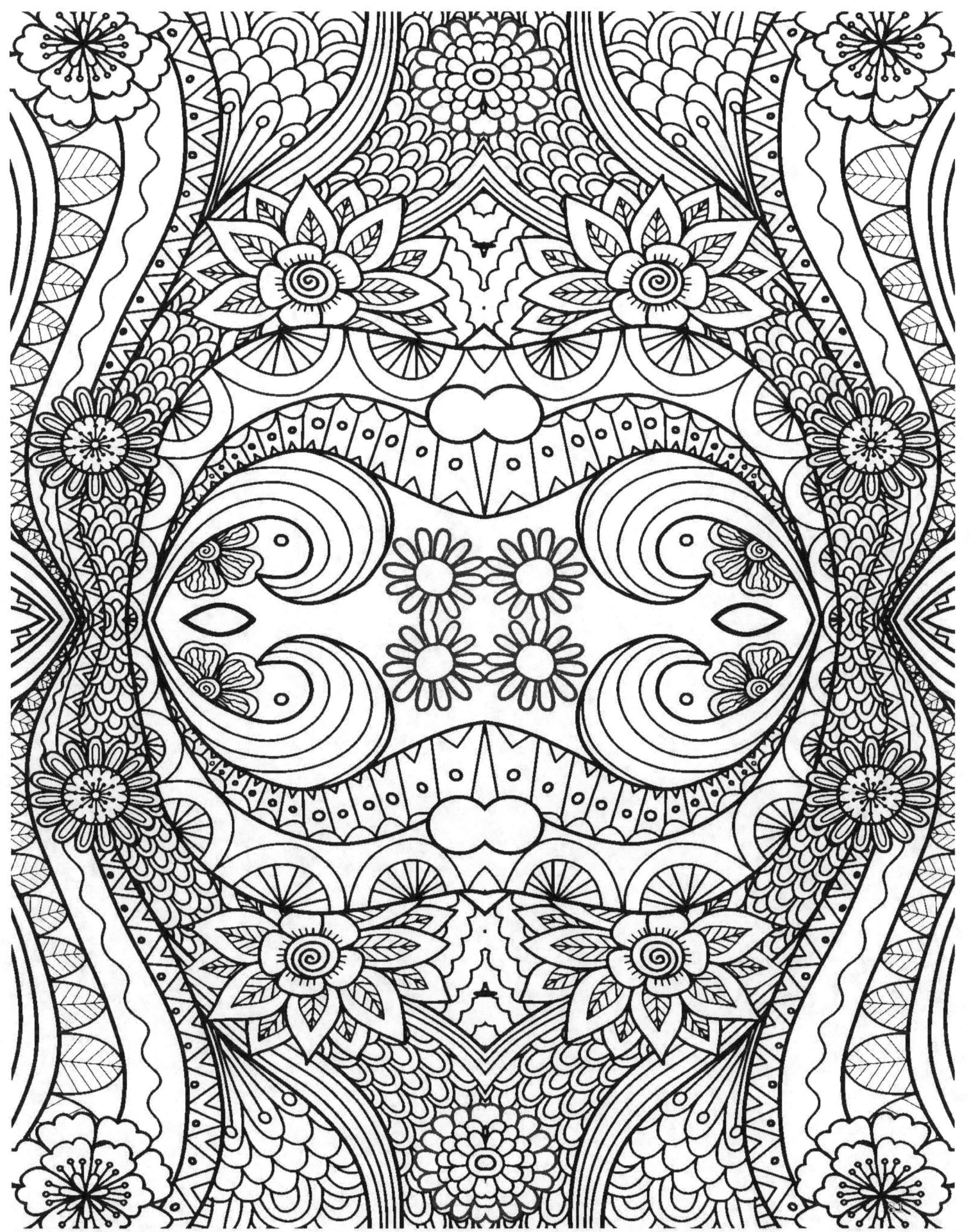

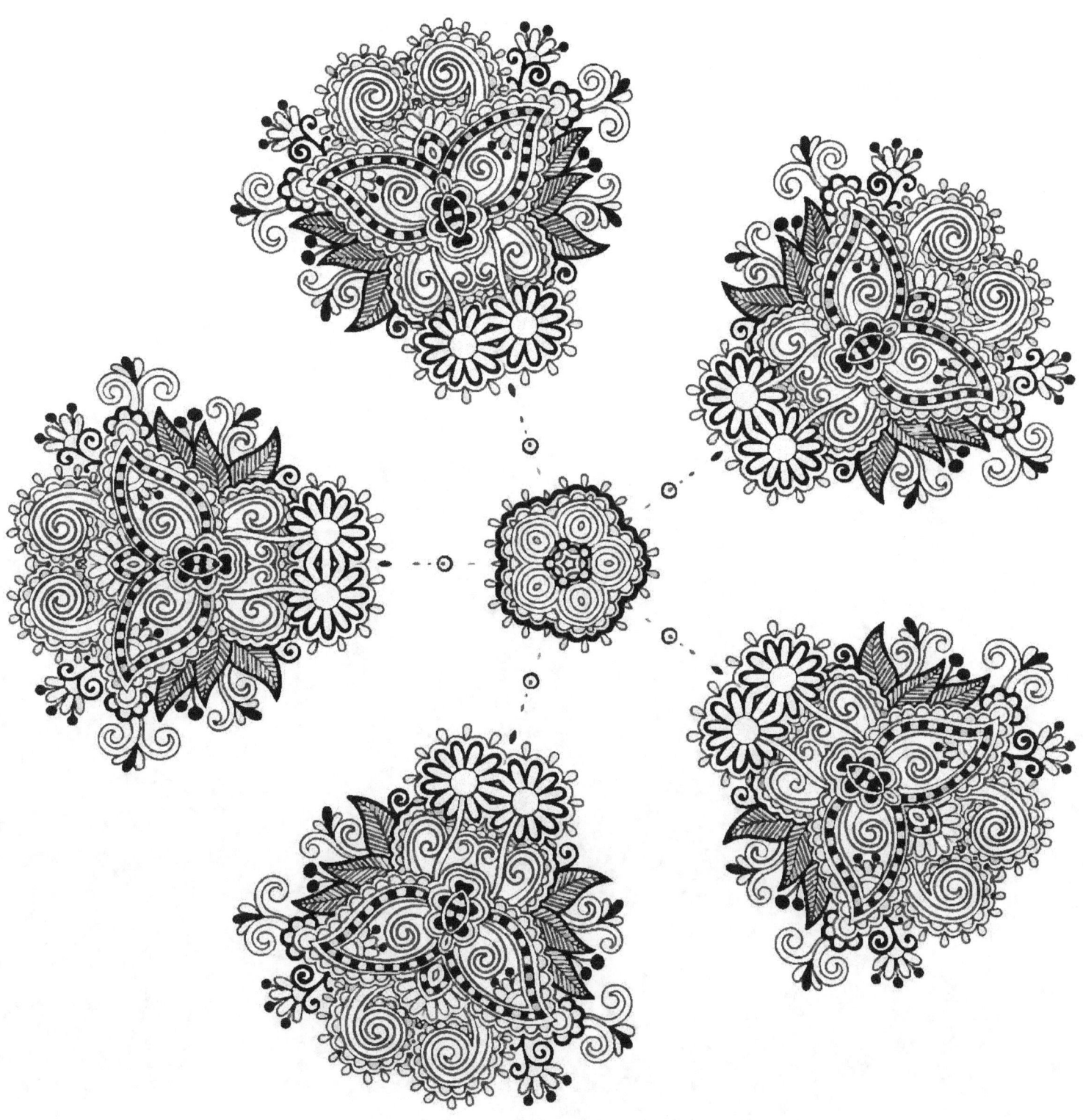

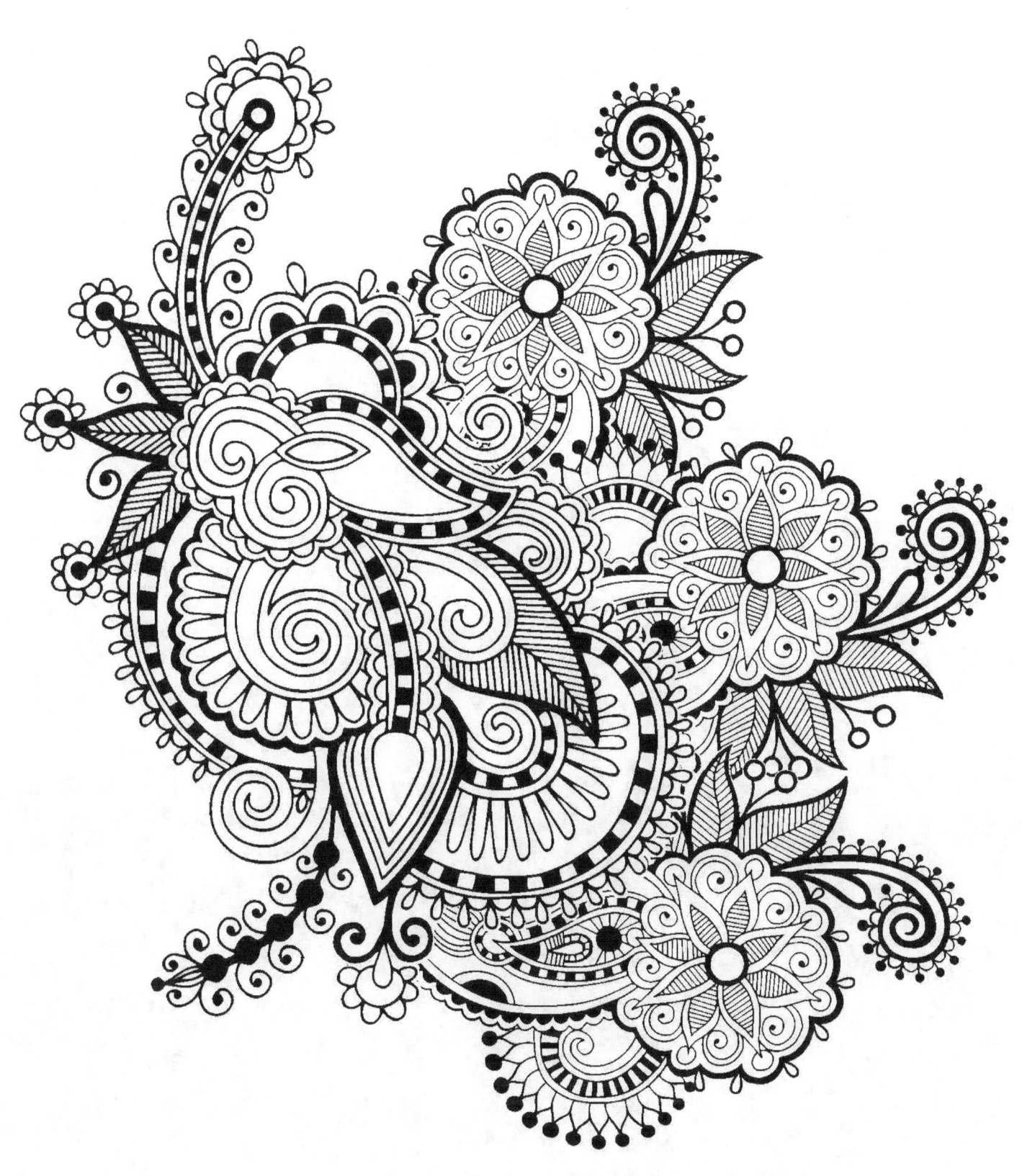

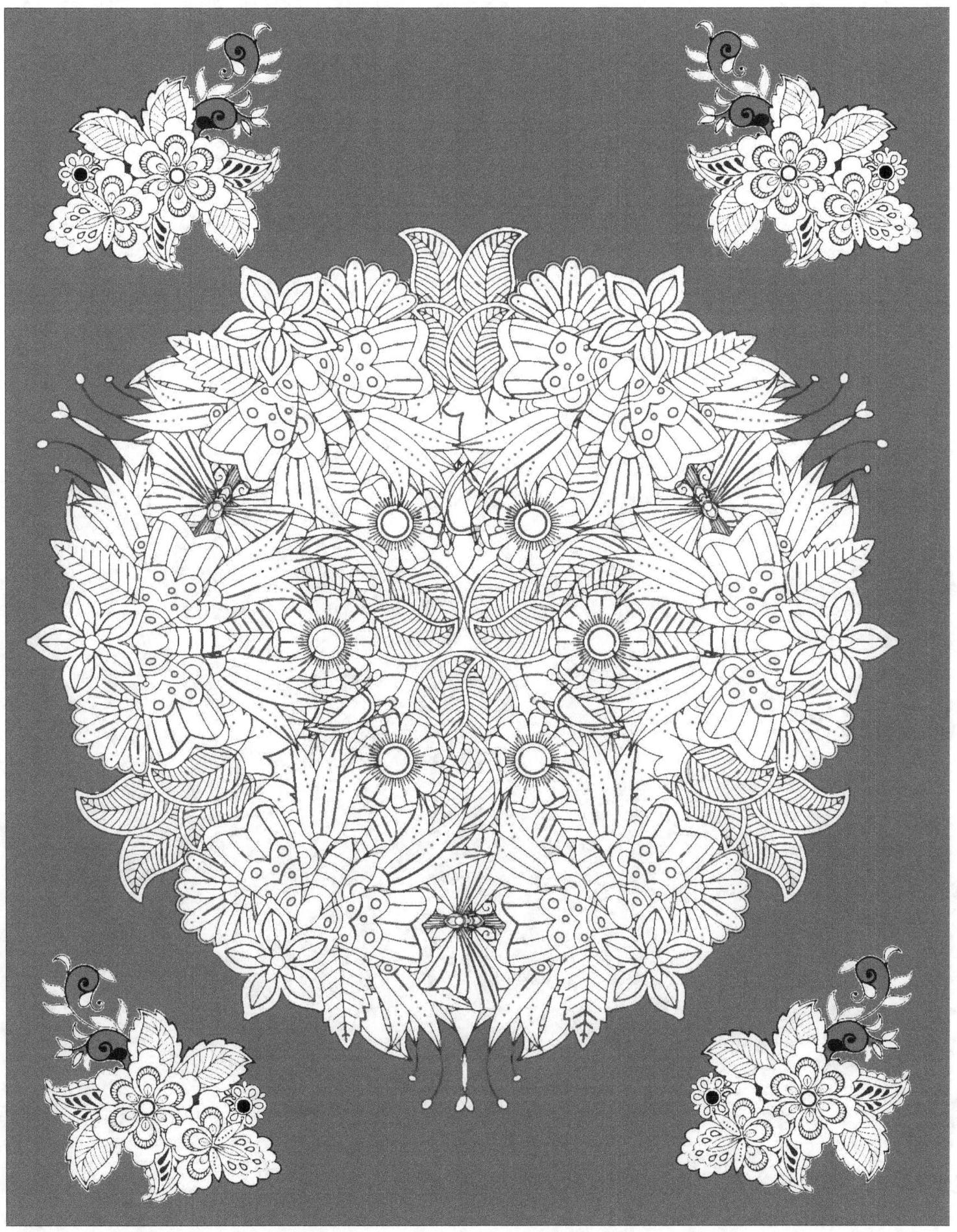

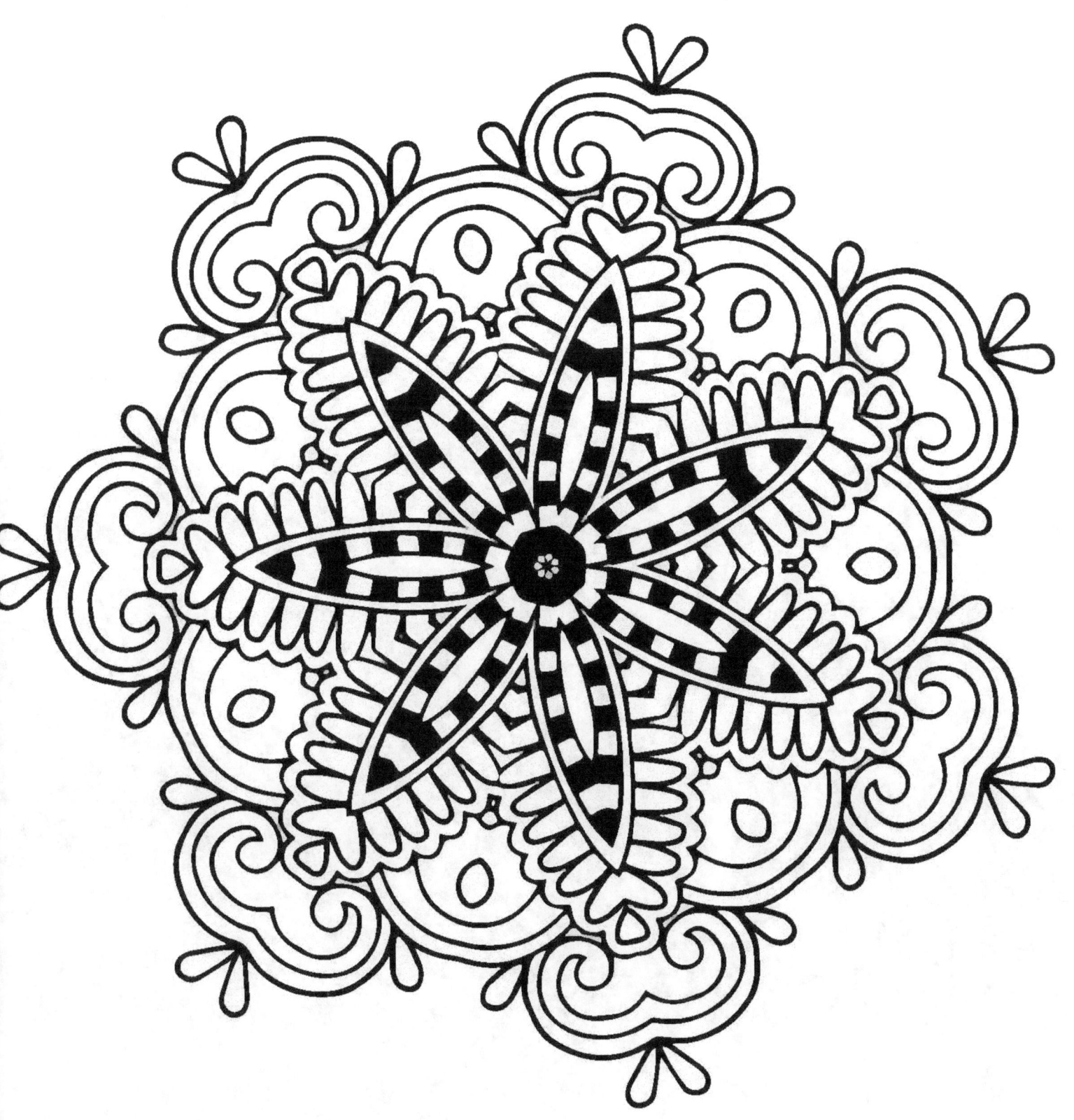

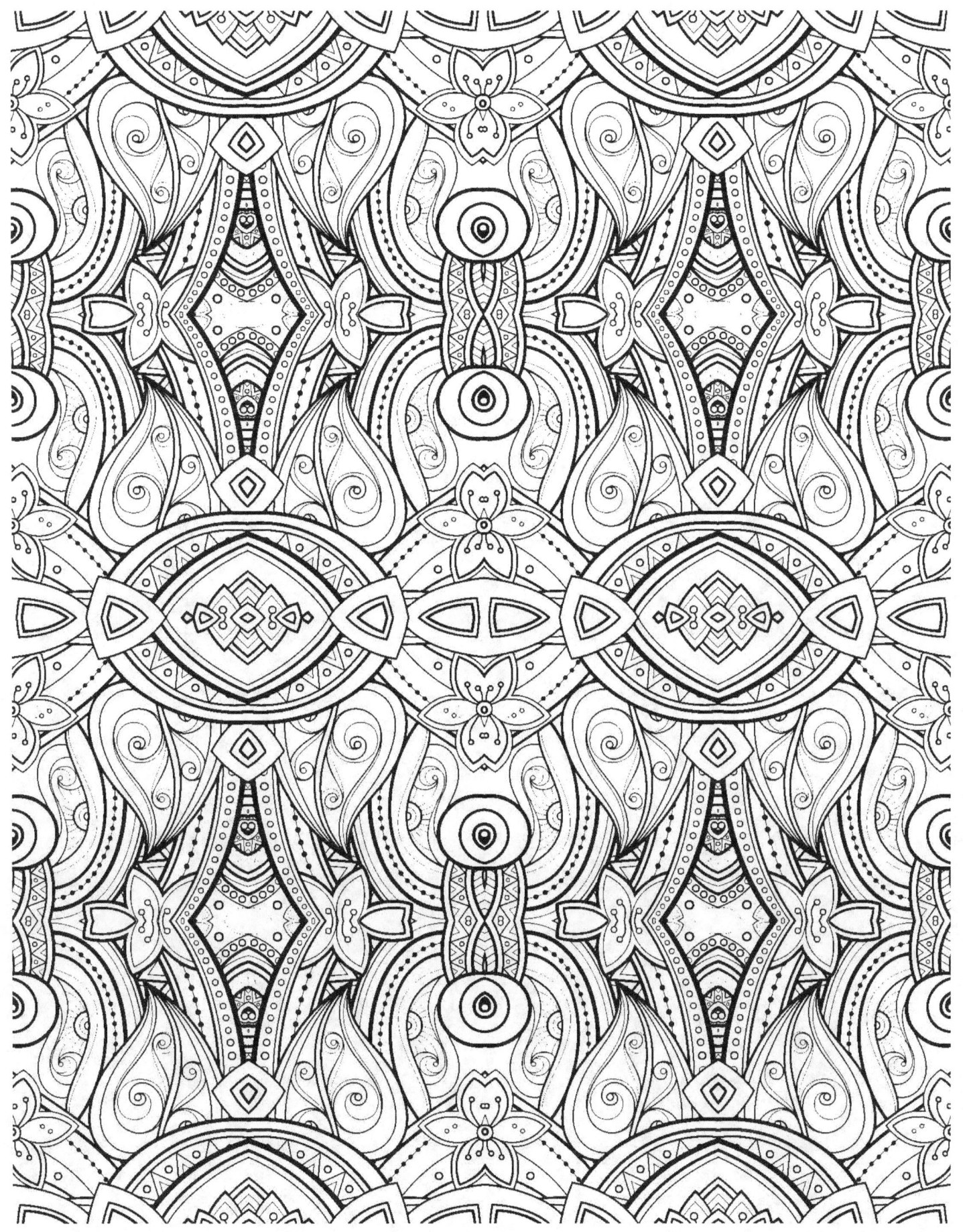

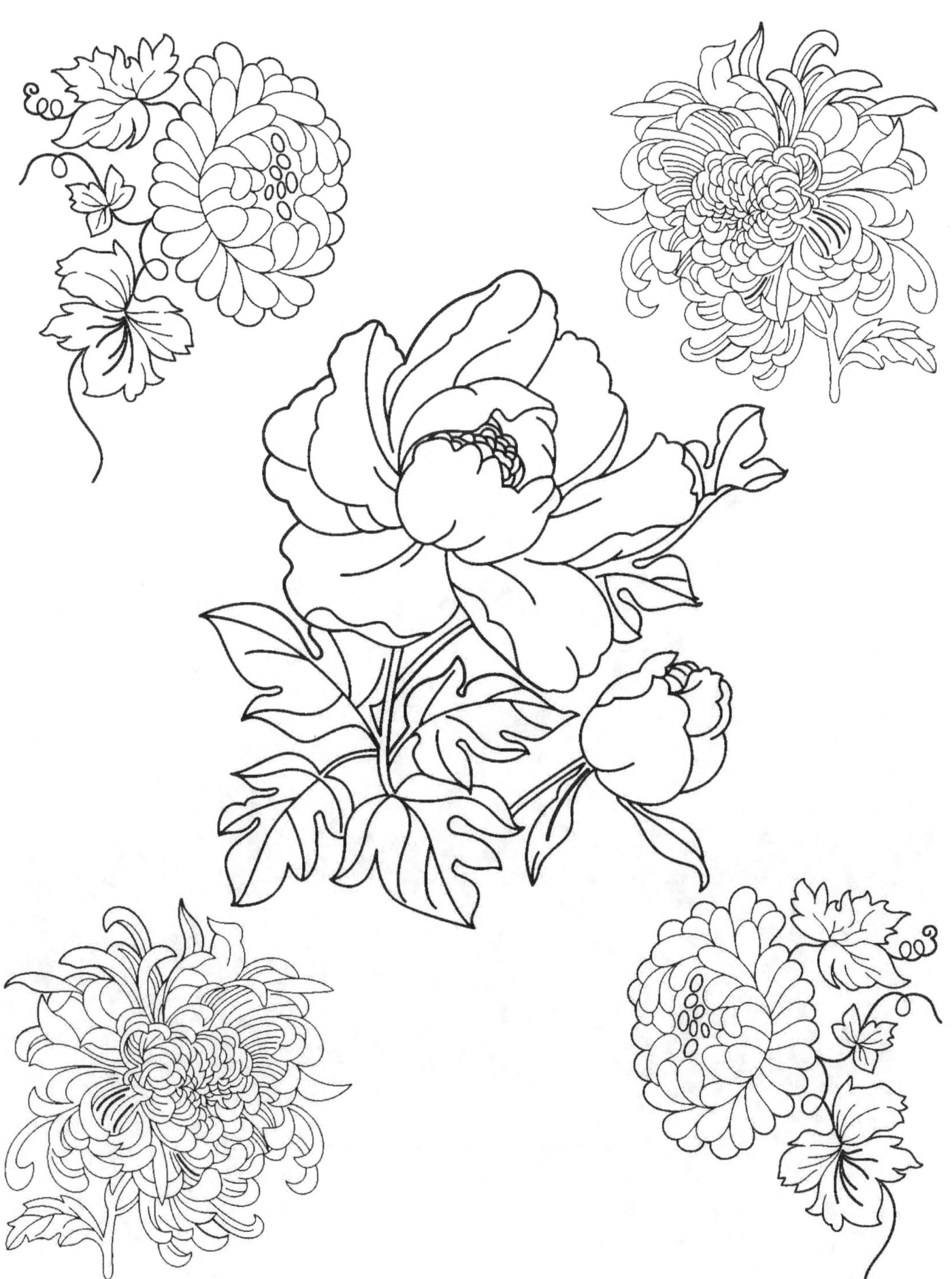

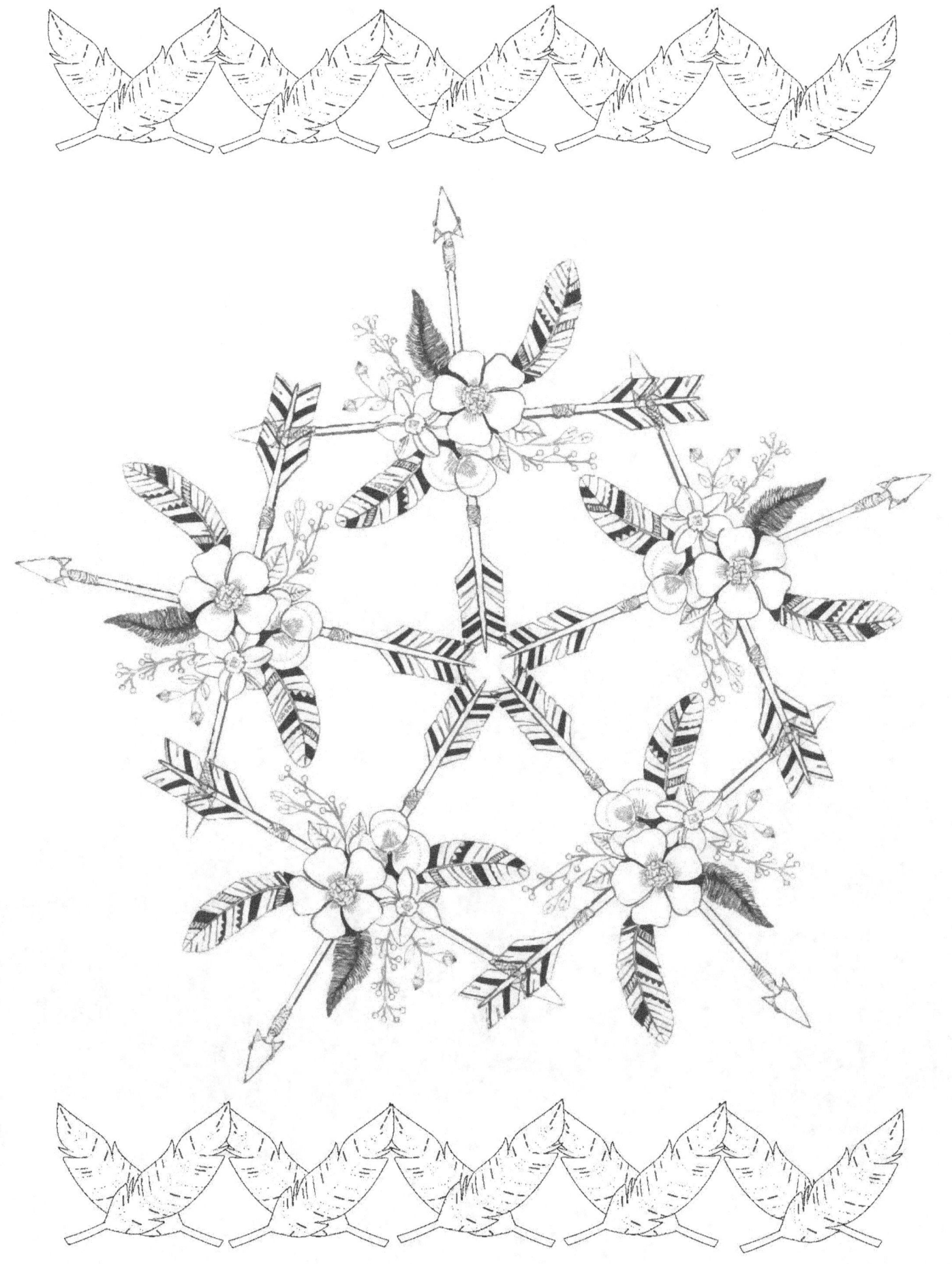

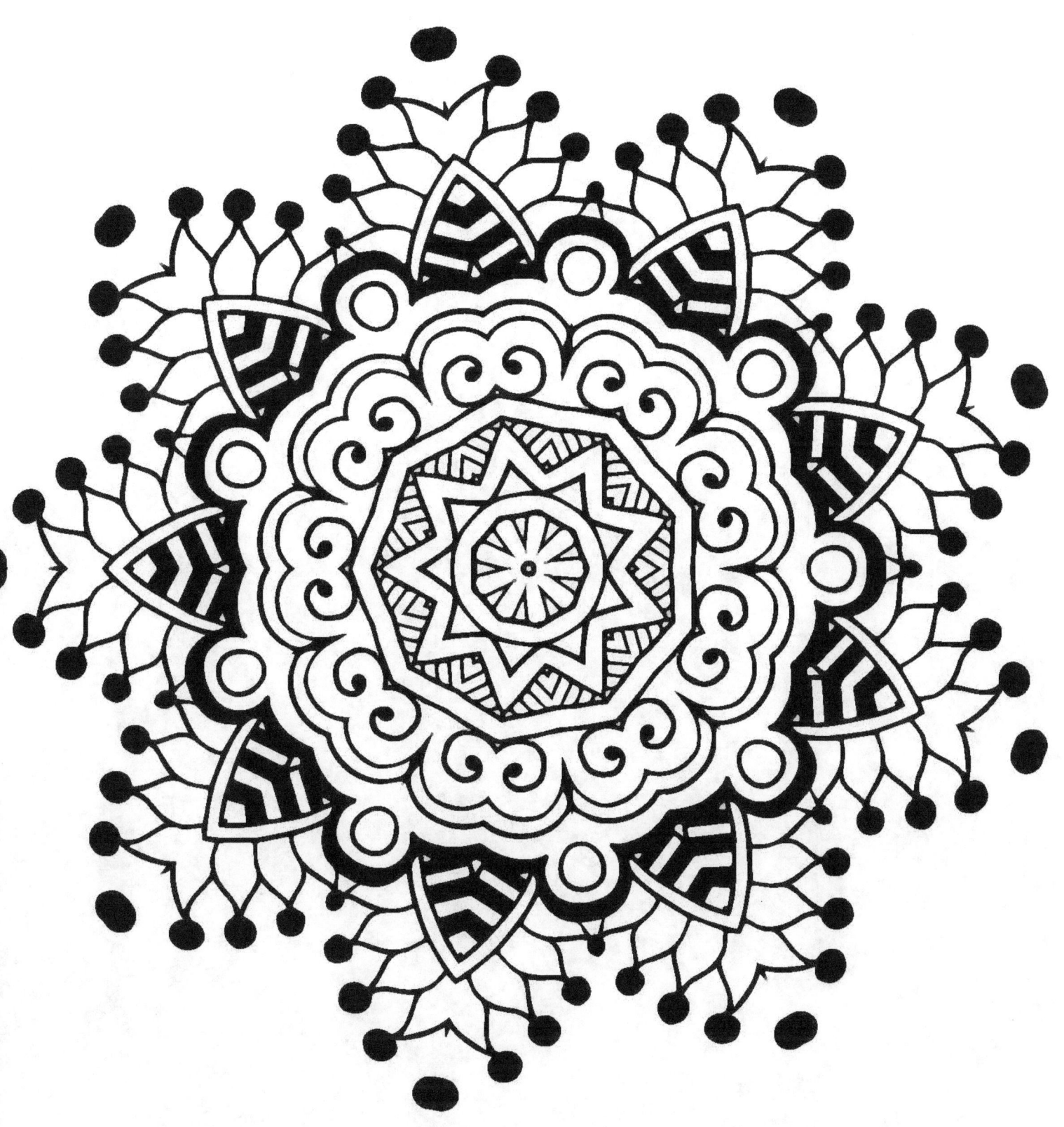

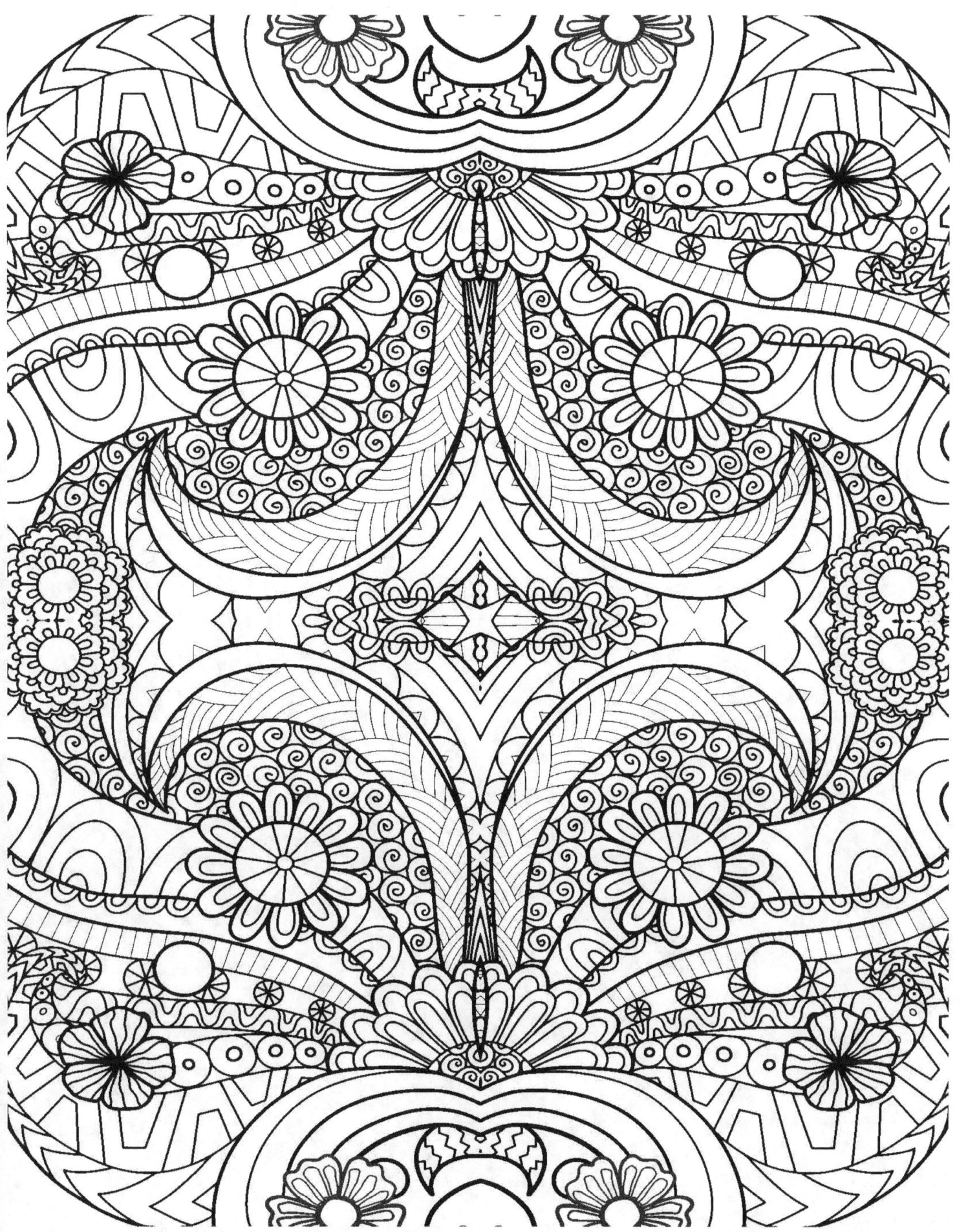

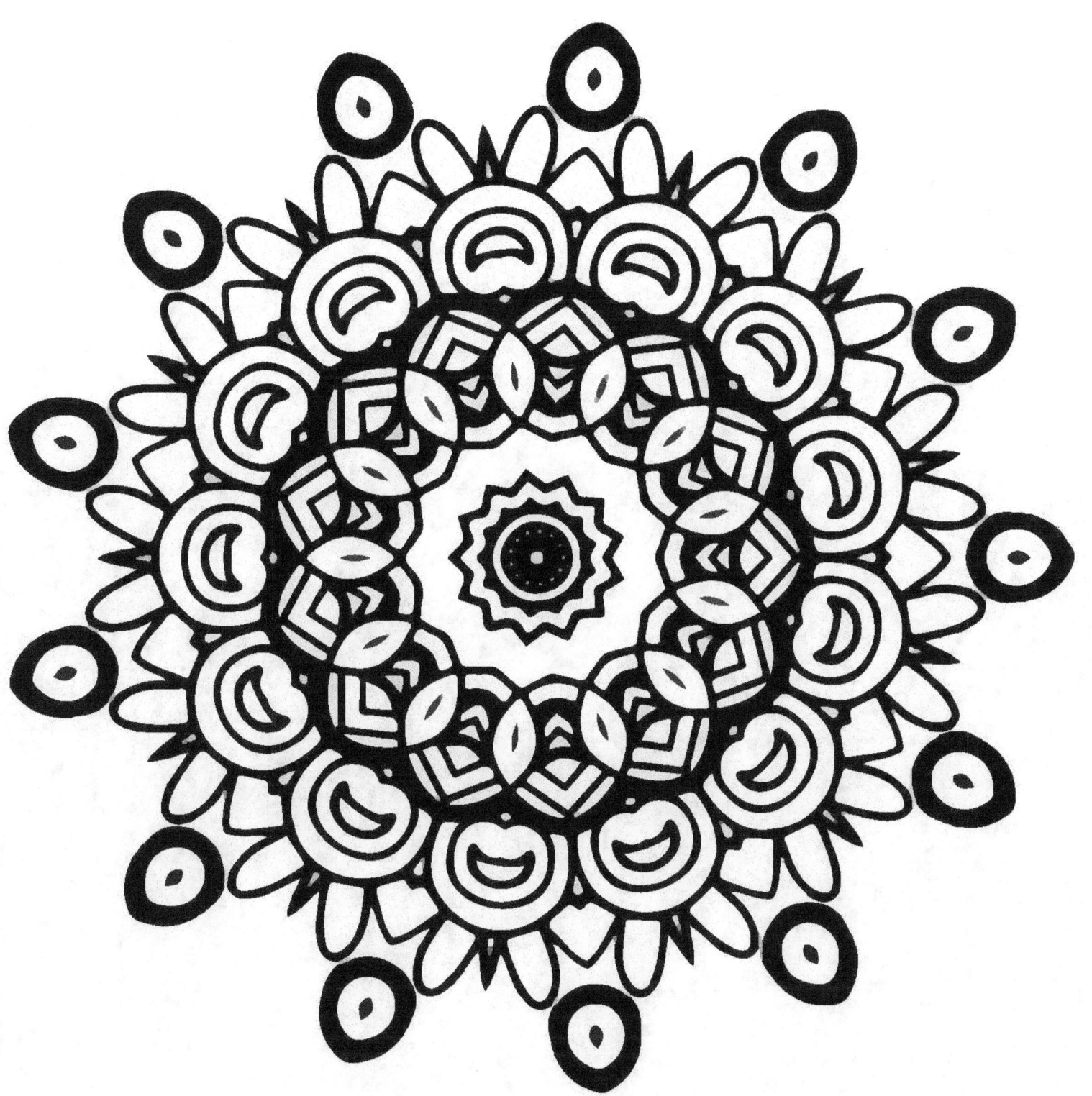

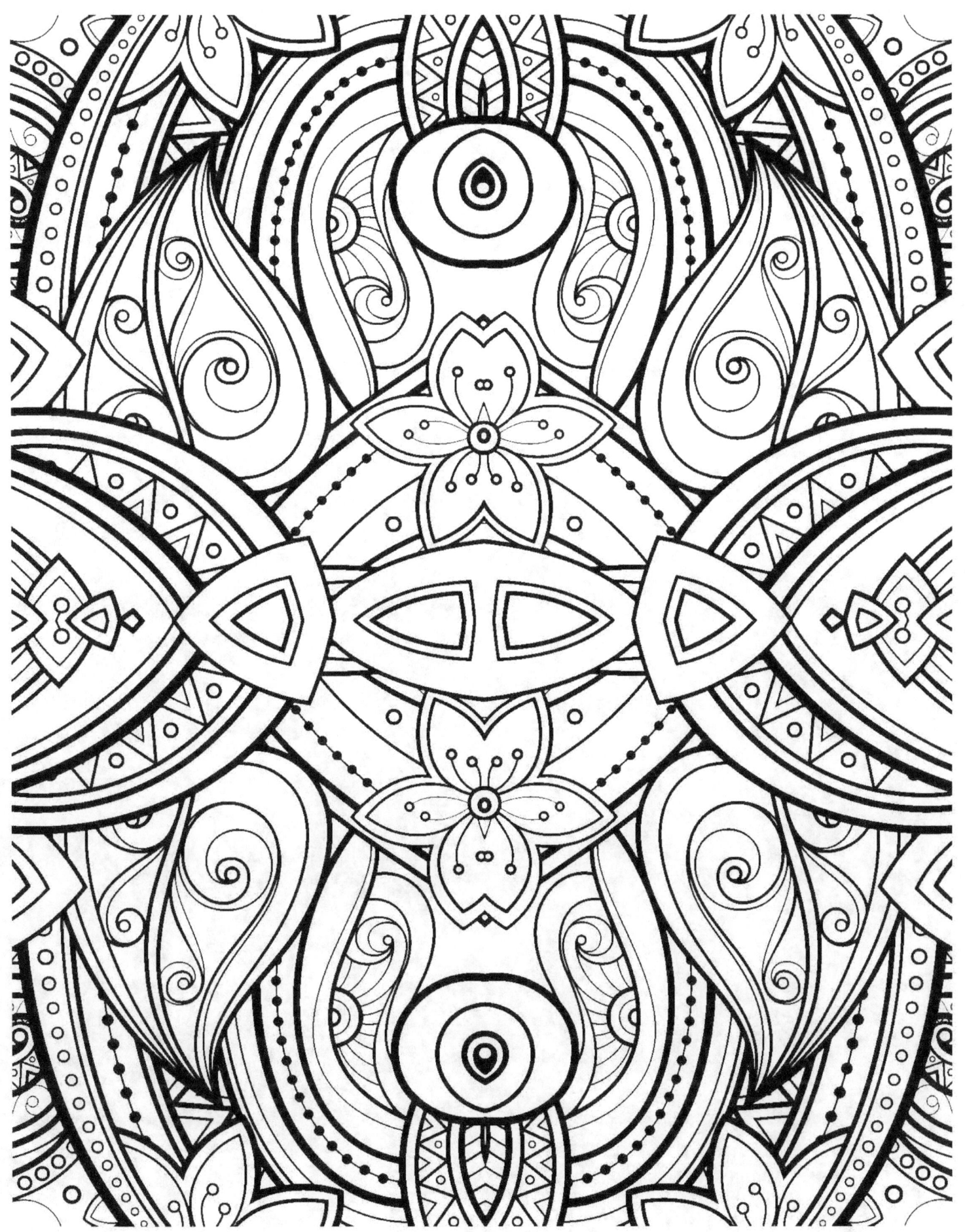

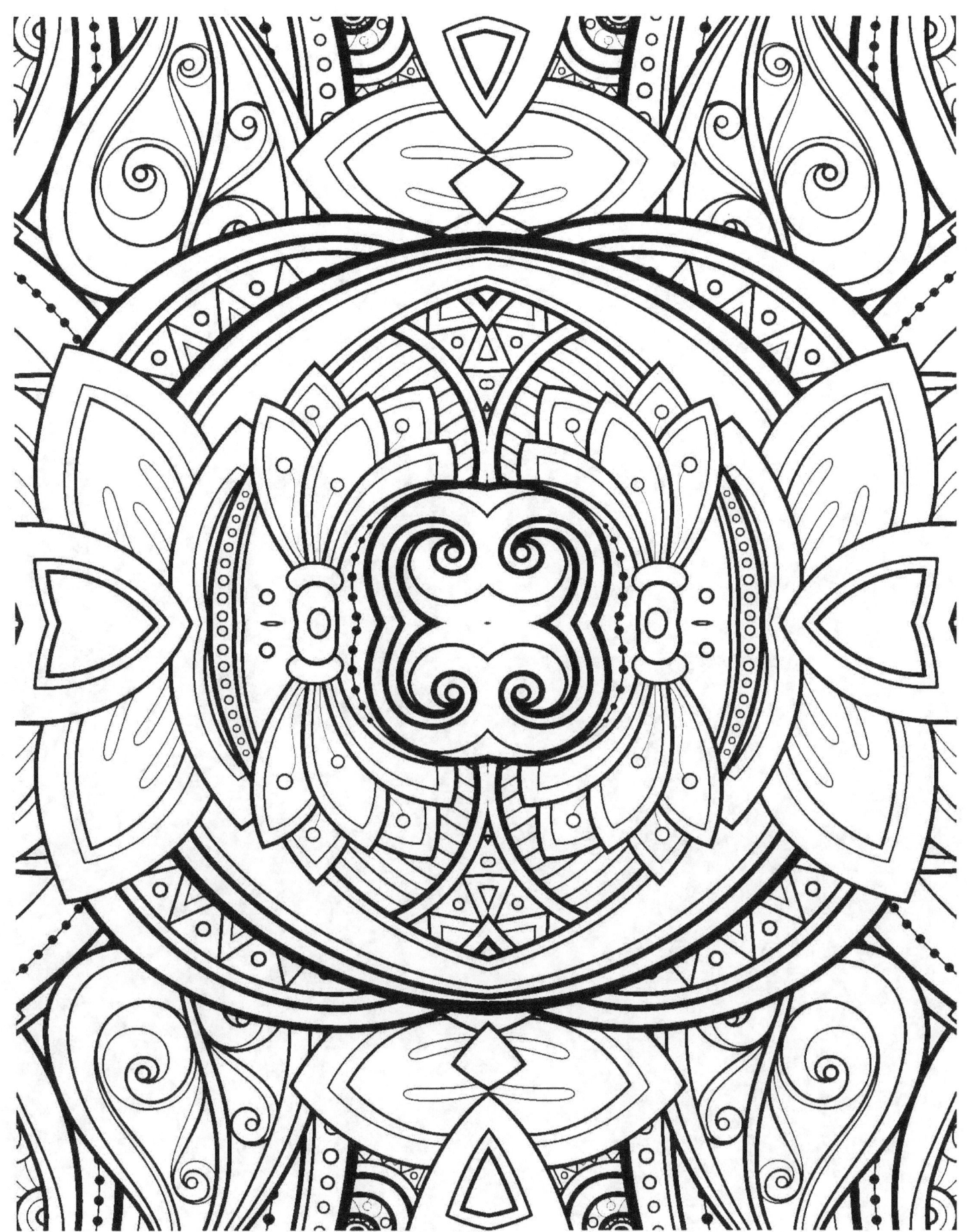

www.ingramcontent.com/pod-product-compliance
Lightning Source LLC
Chambersburg PA
CBHW081001170526
45158CB00010B/2861